Tractor Coloring Bc

MW00901572

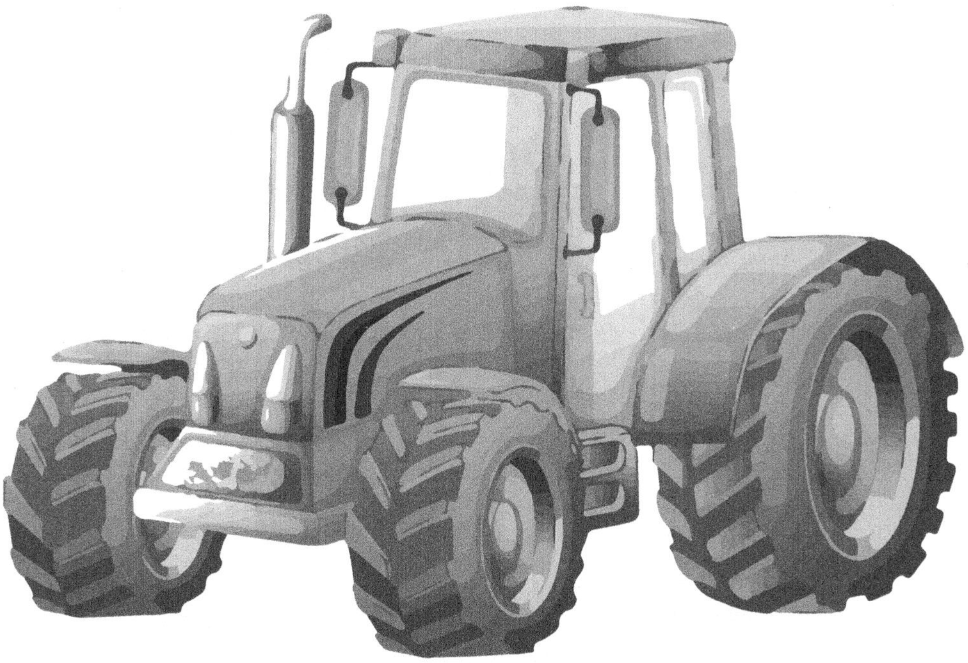

This Book Belong To

....

....

....

....

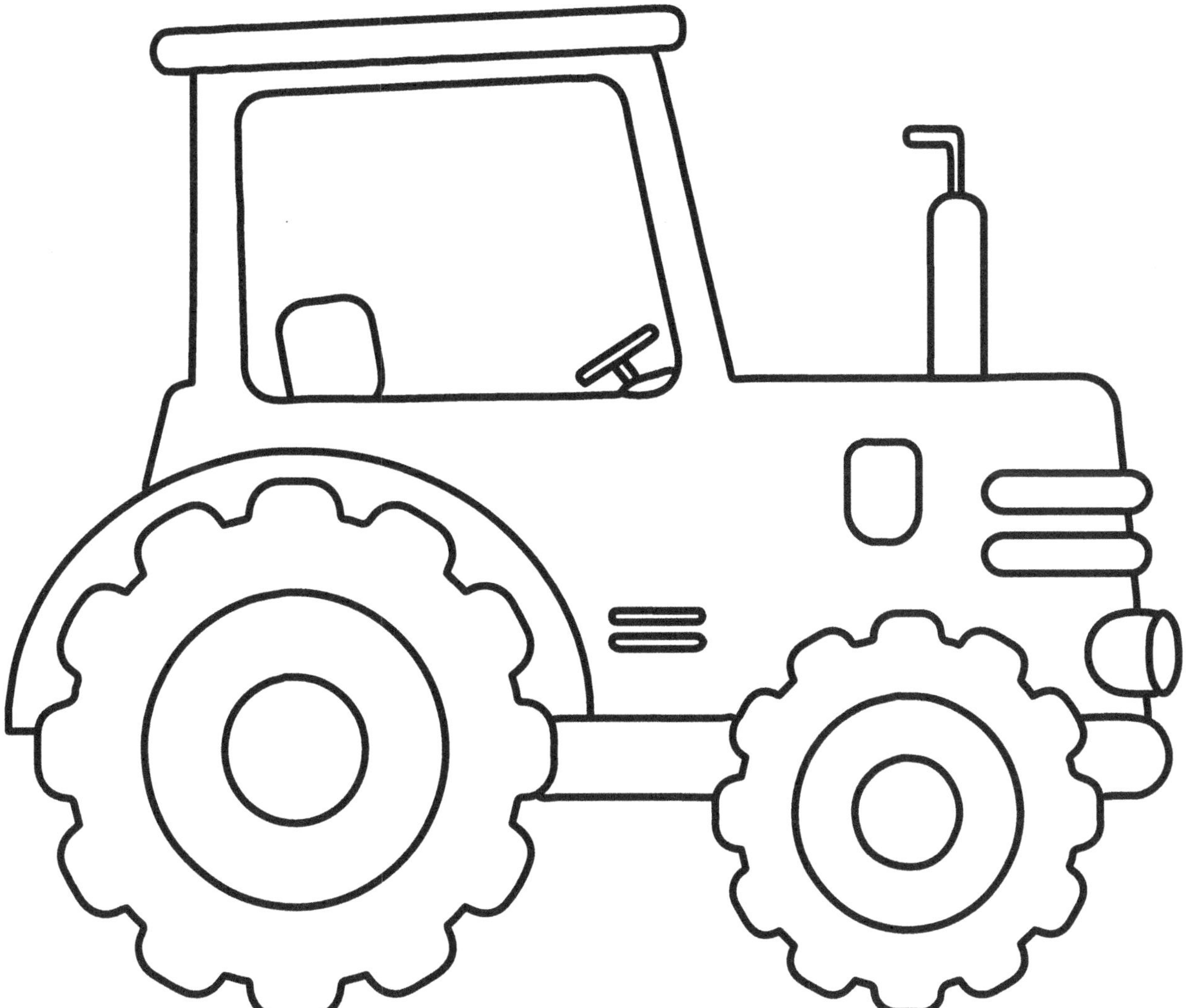

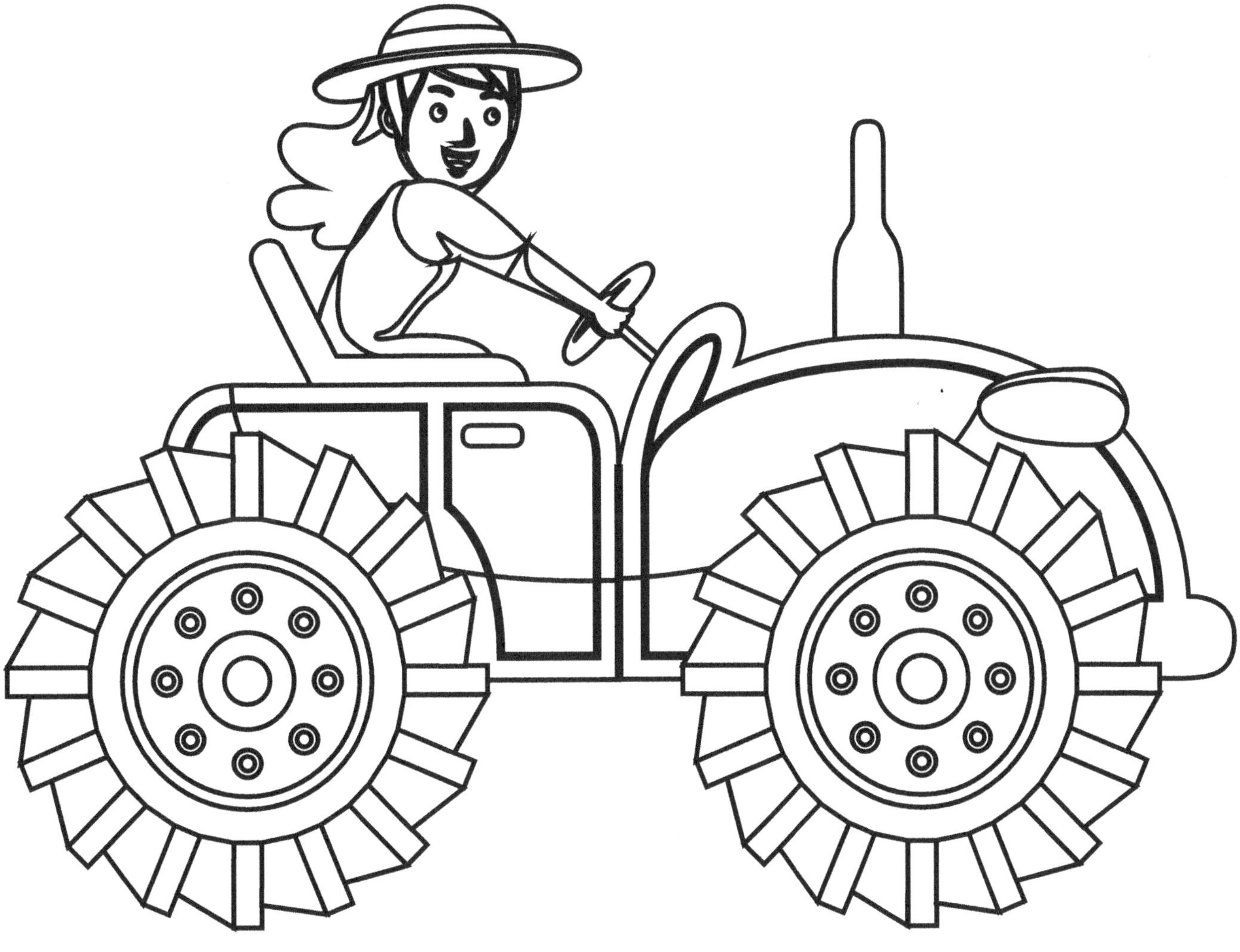

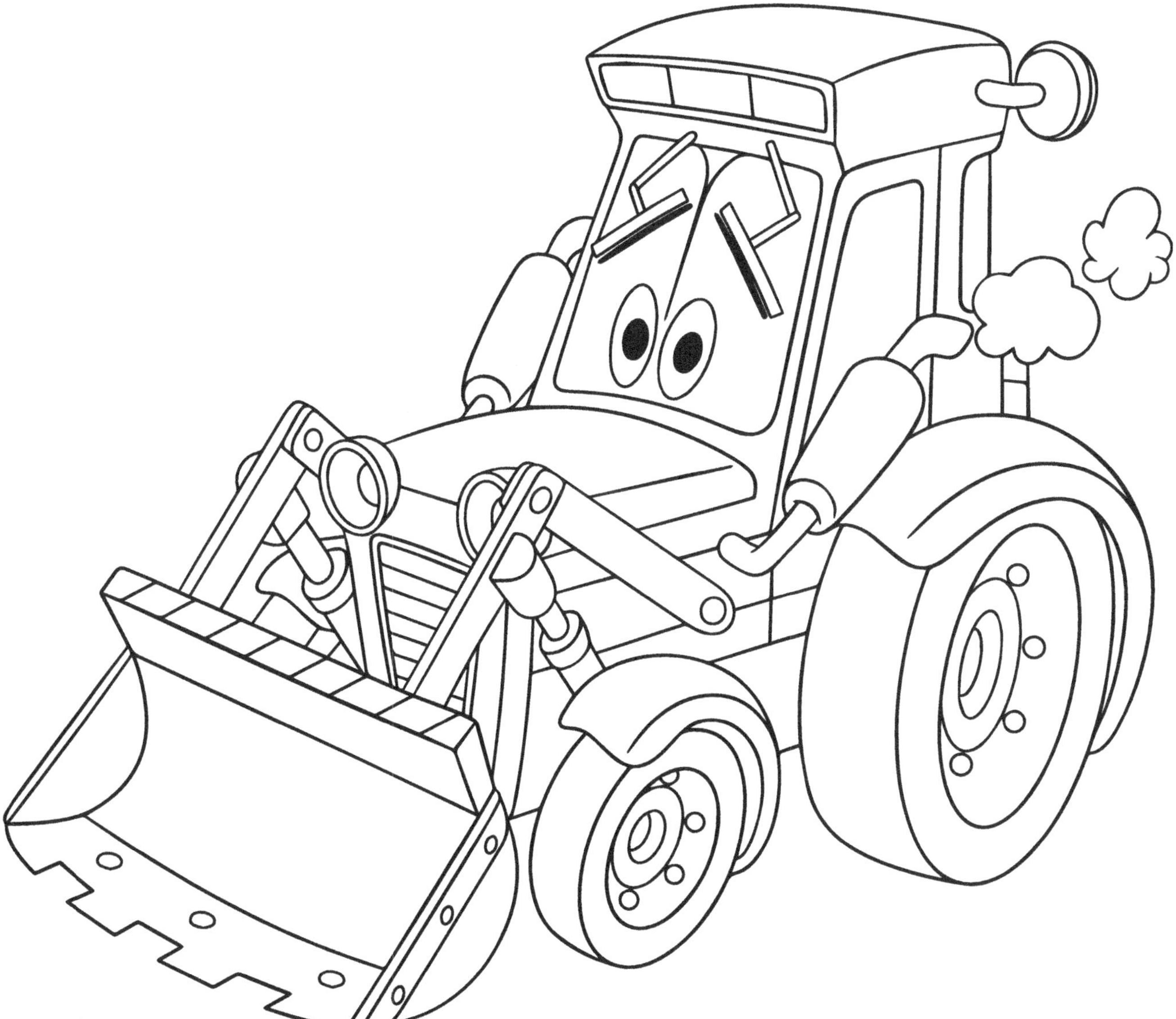

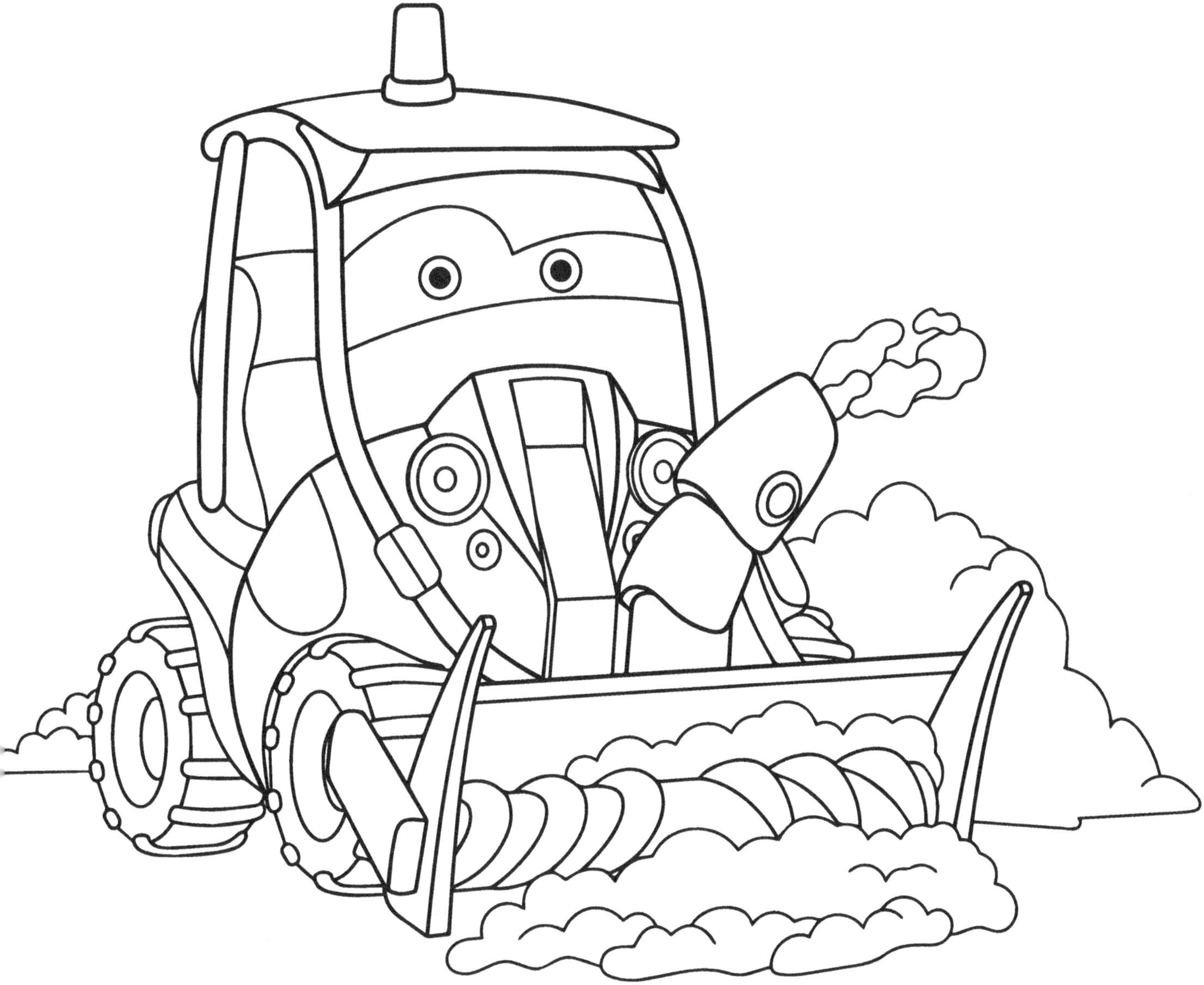

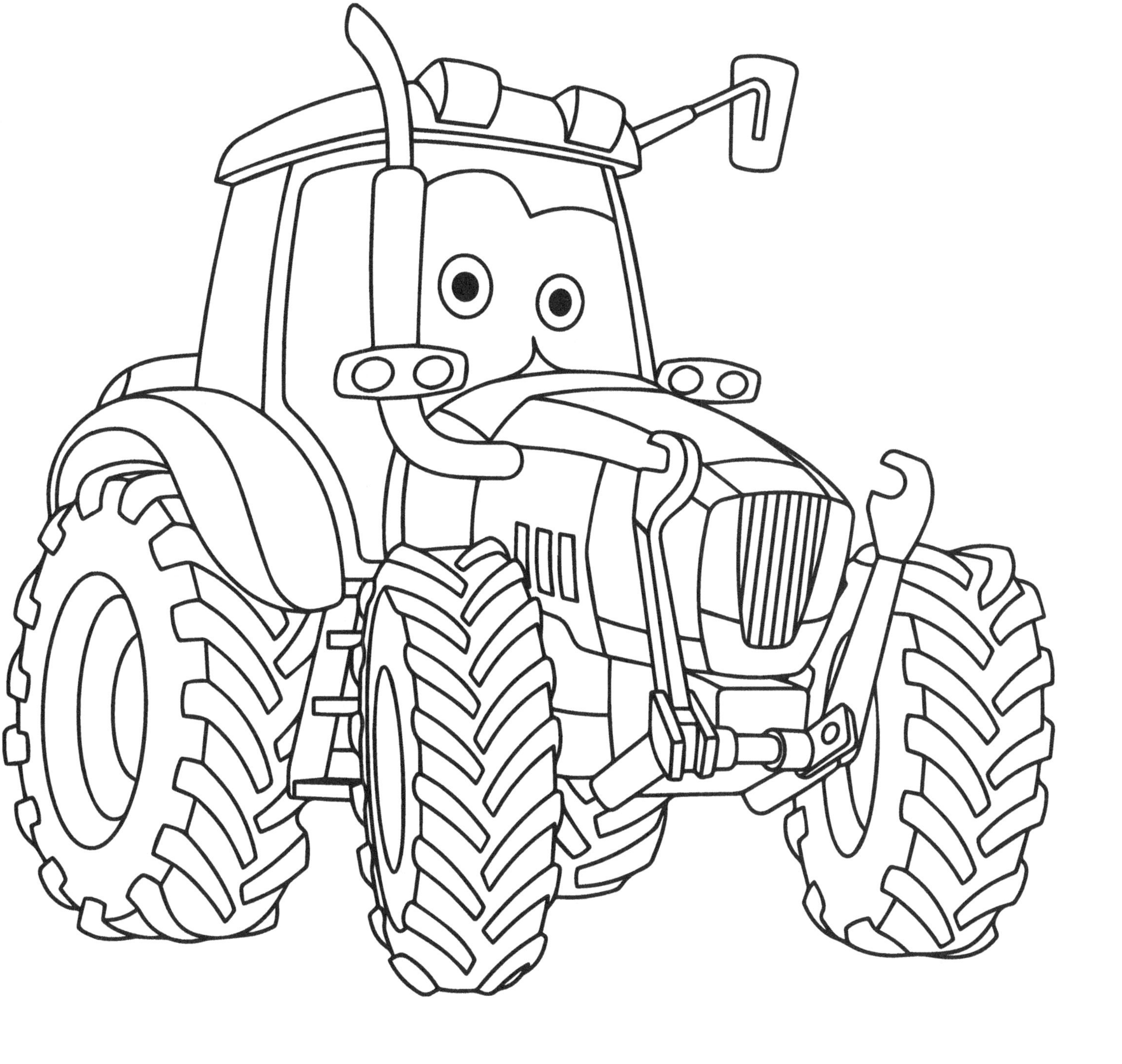

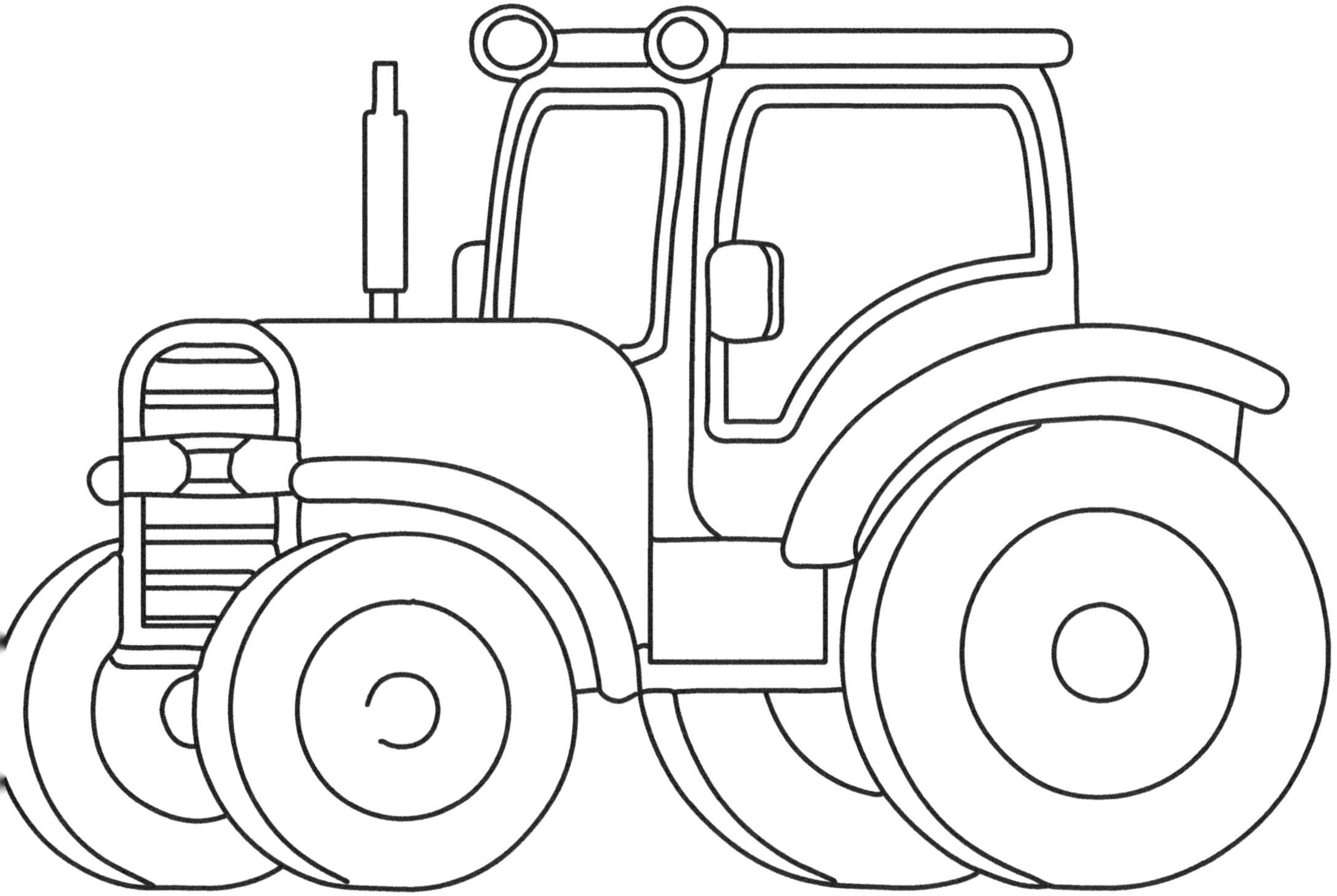

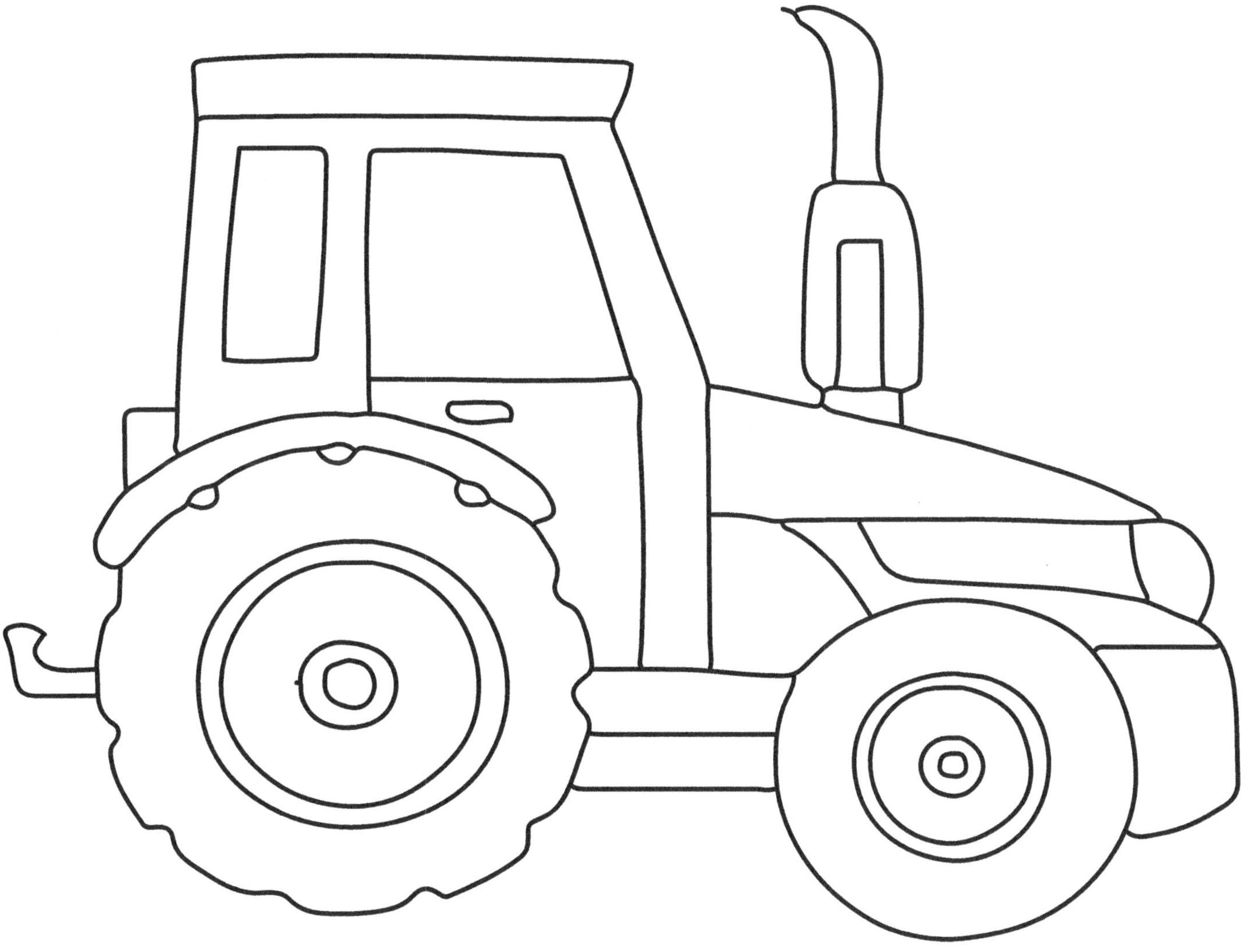

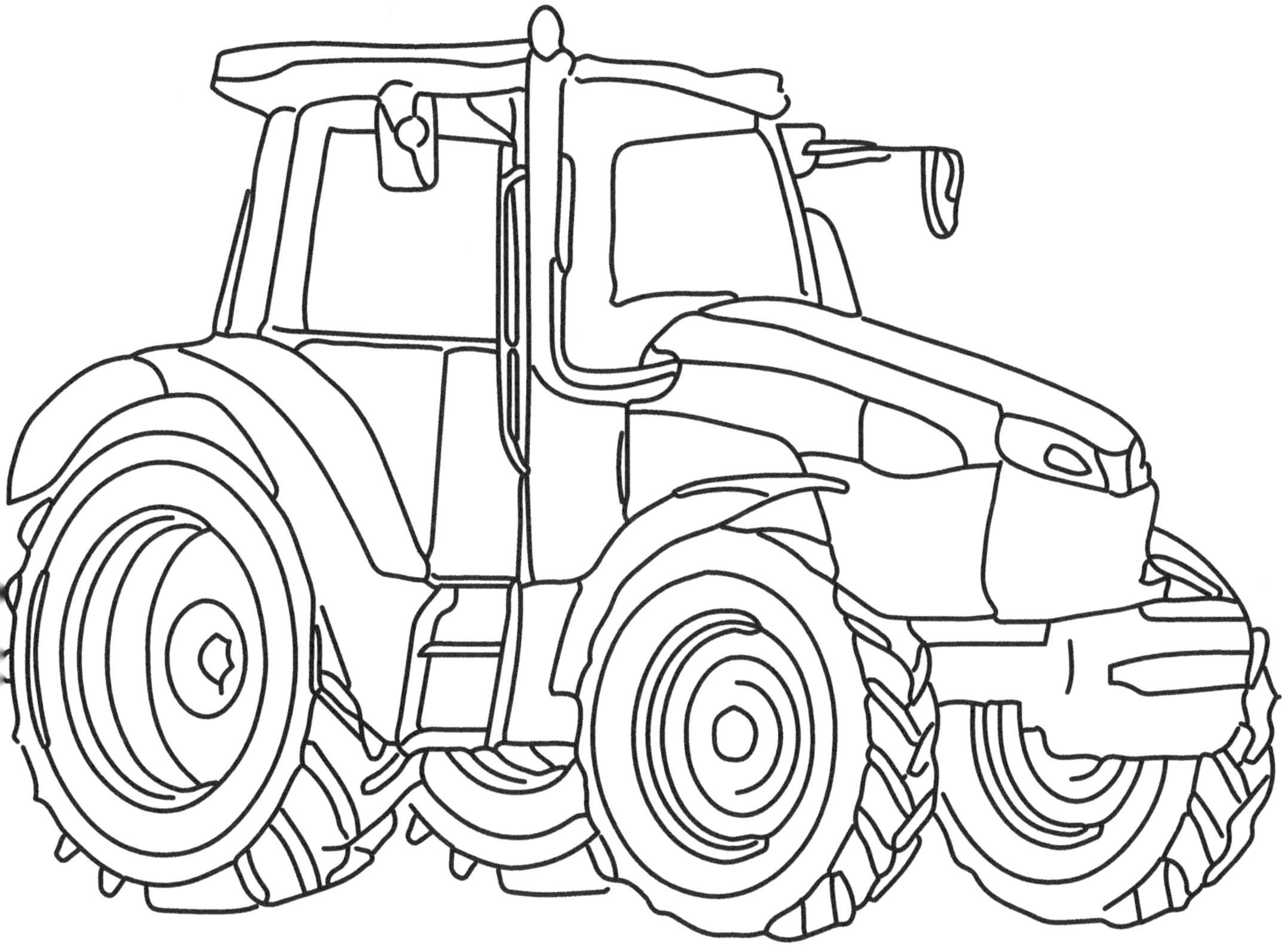

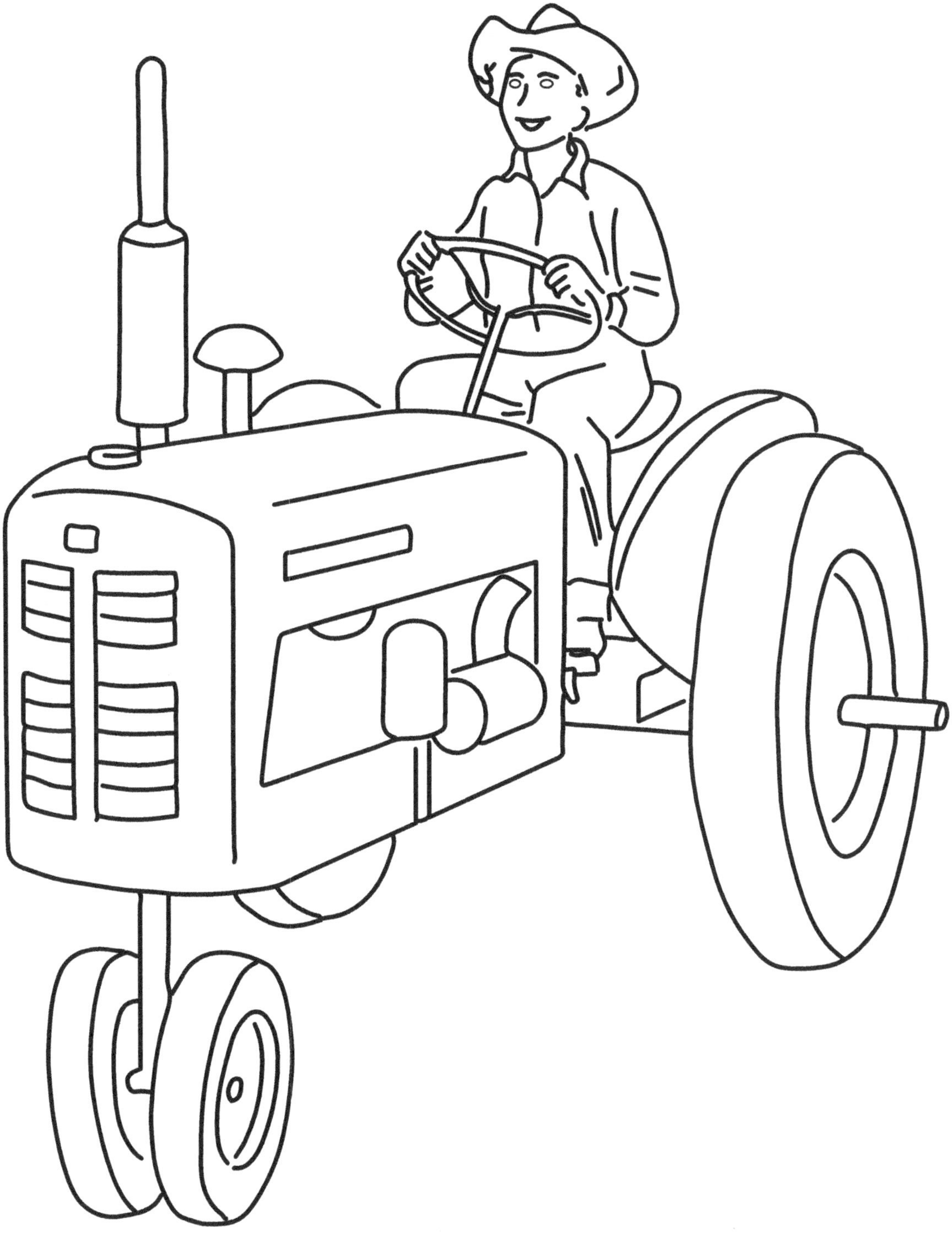

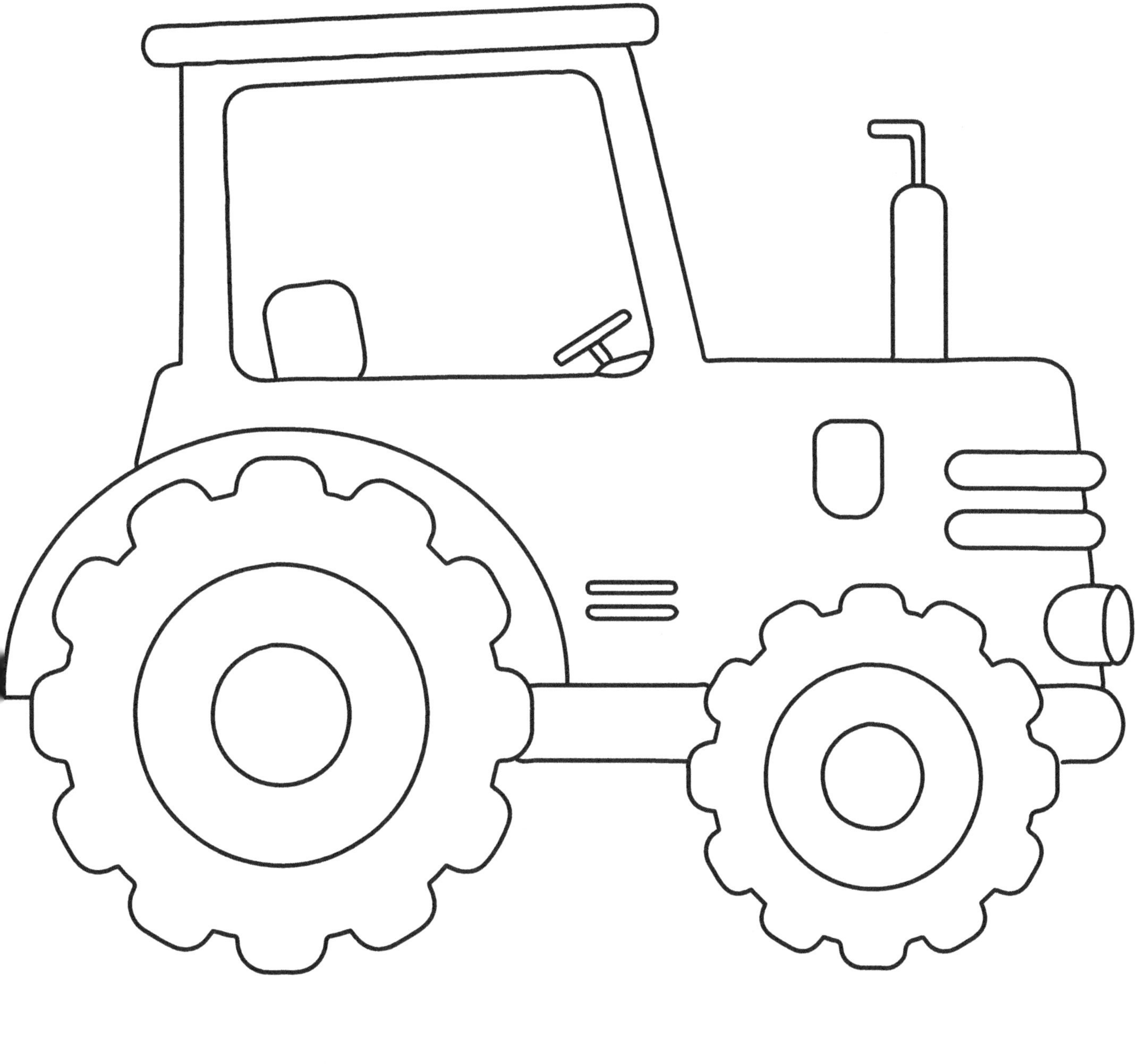

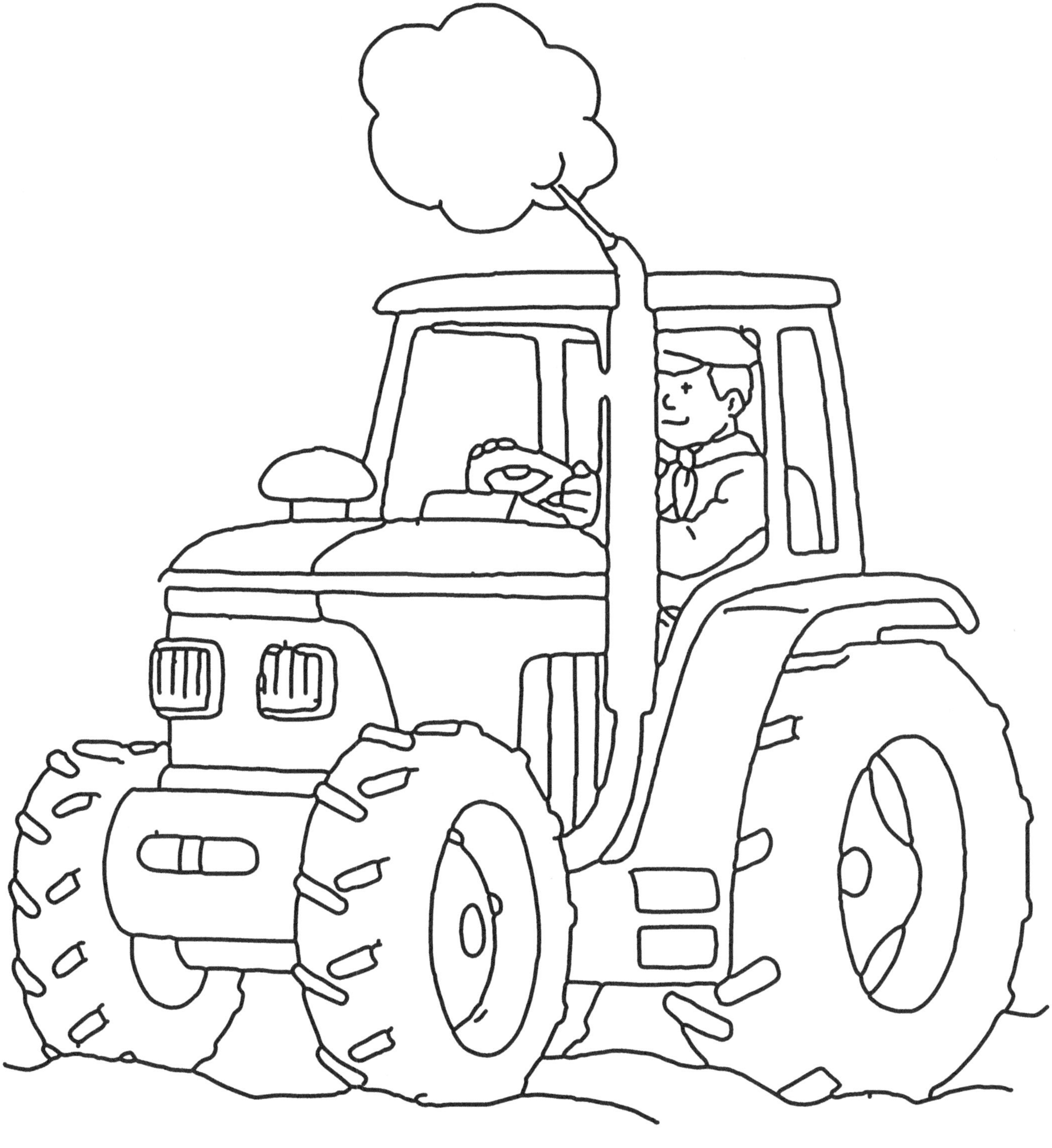

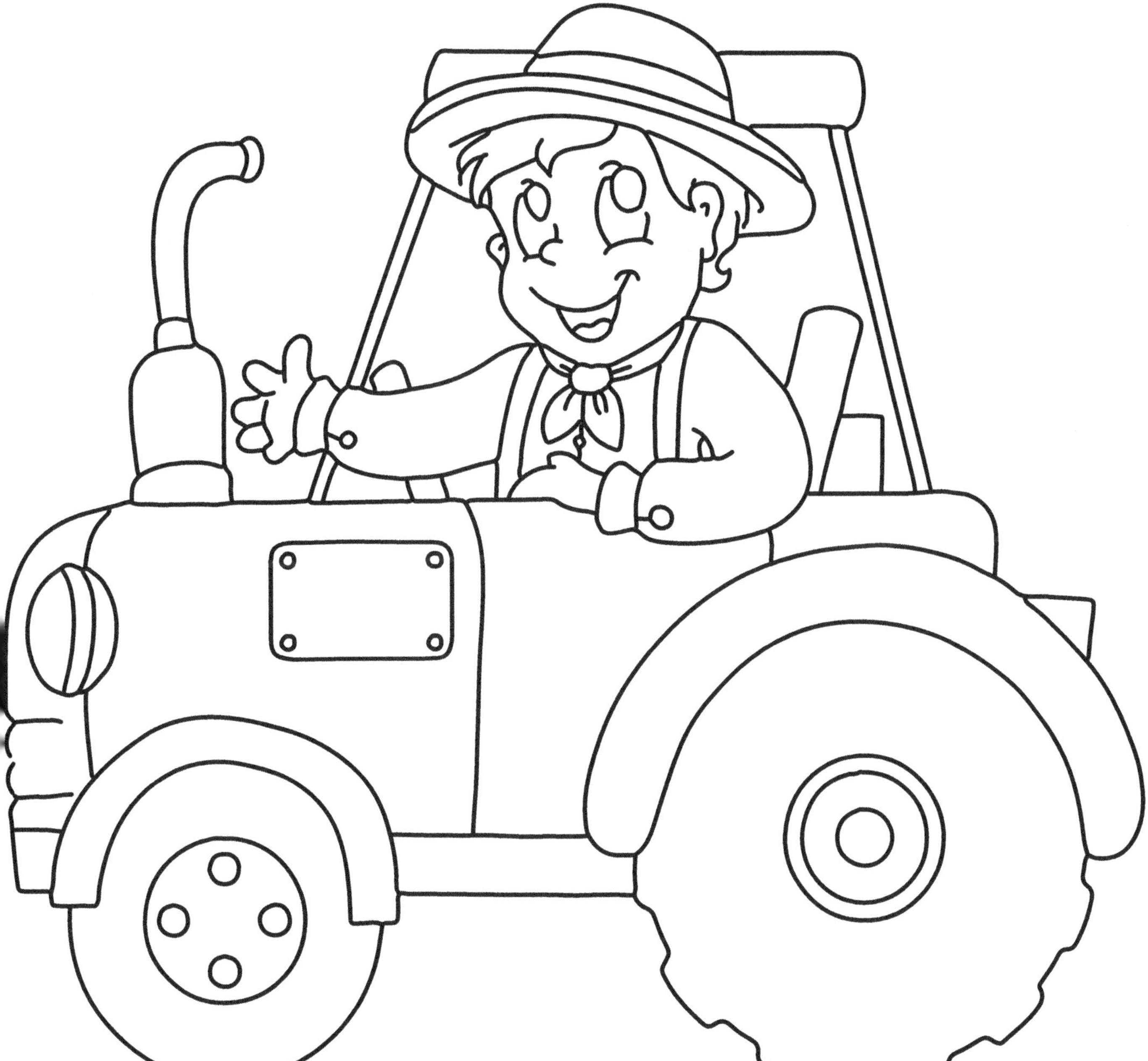

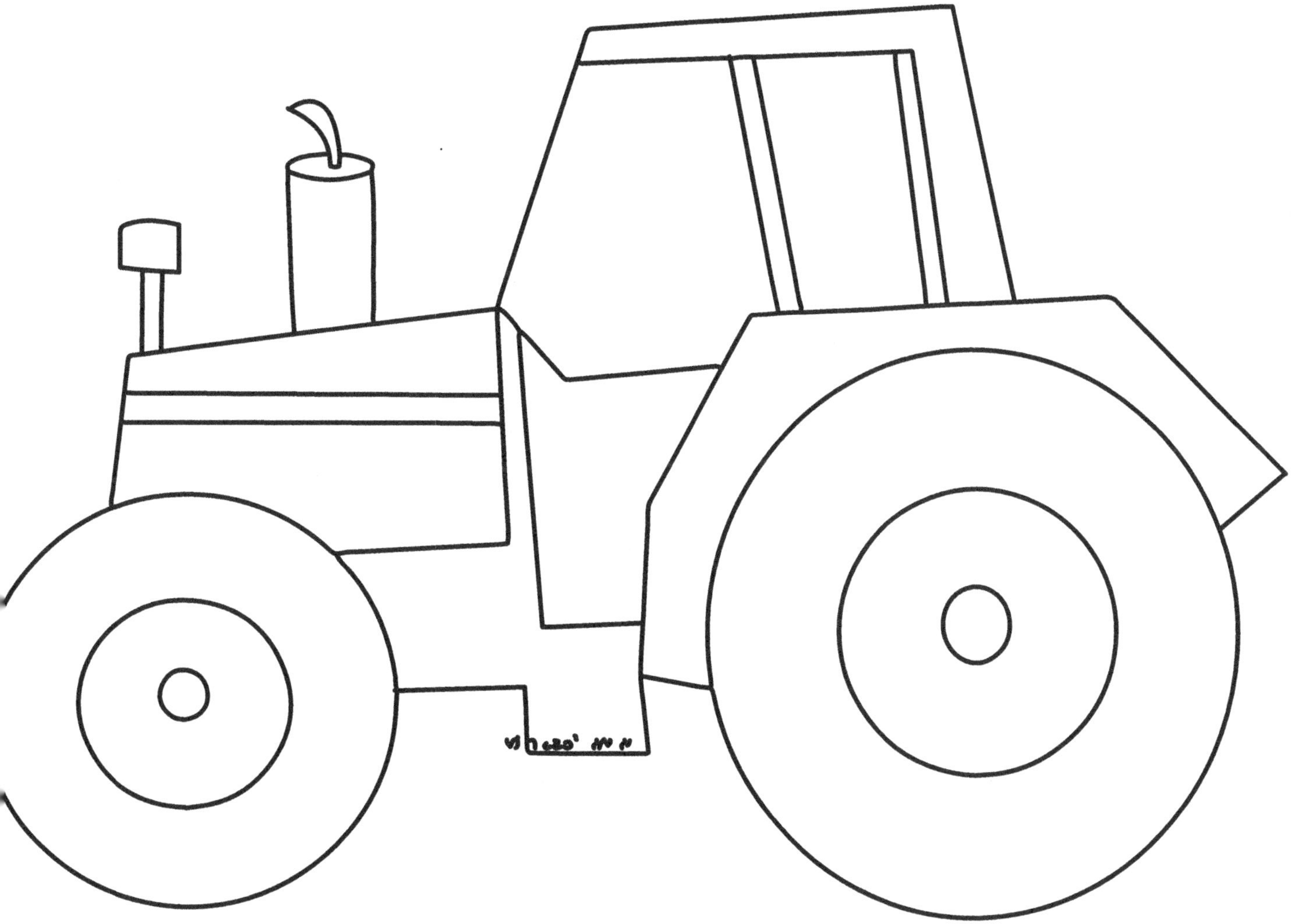

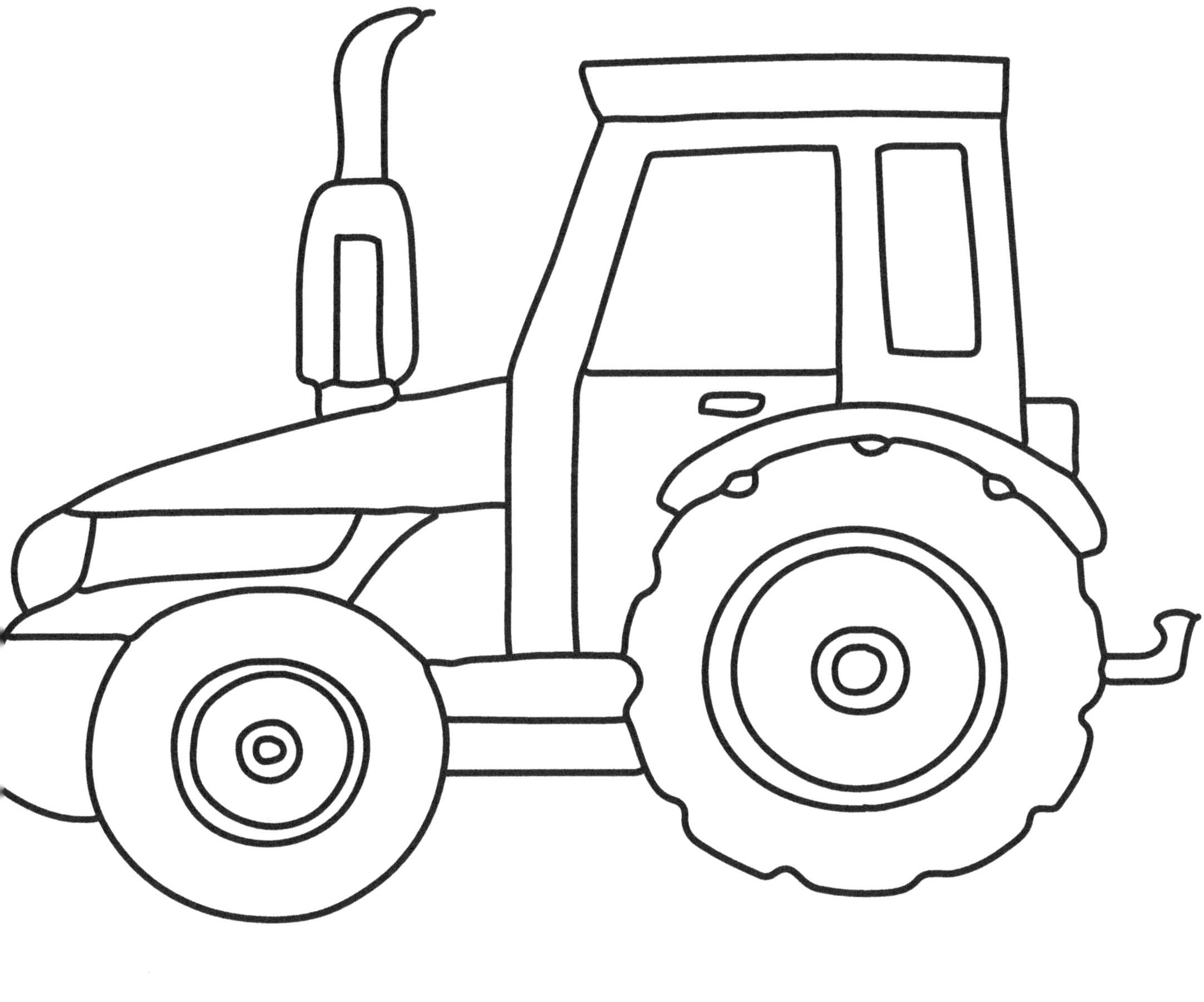

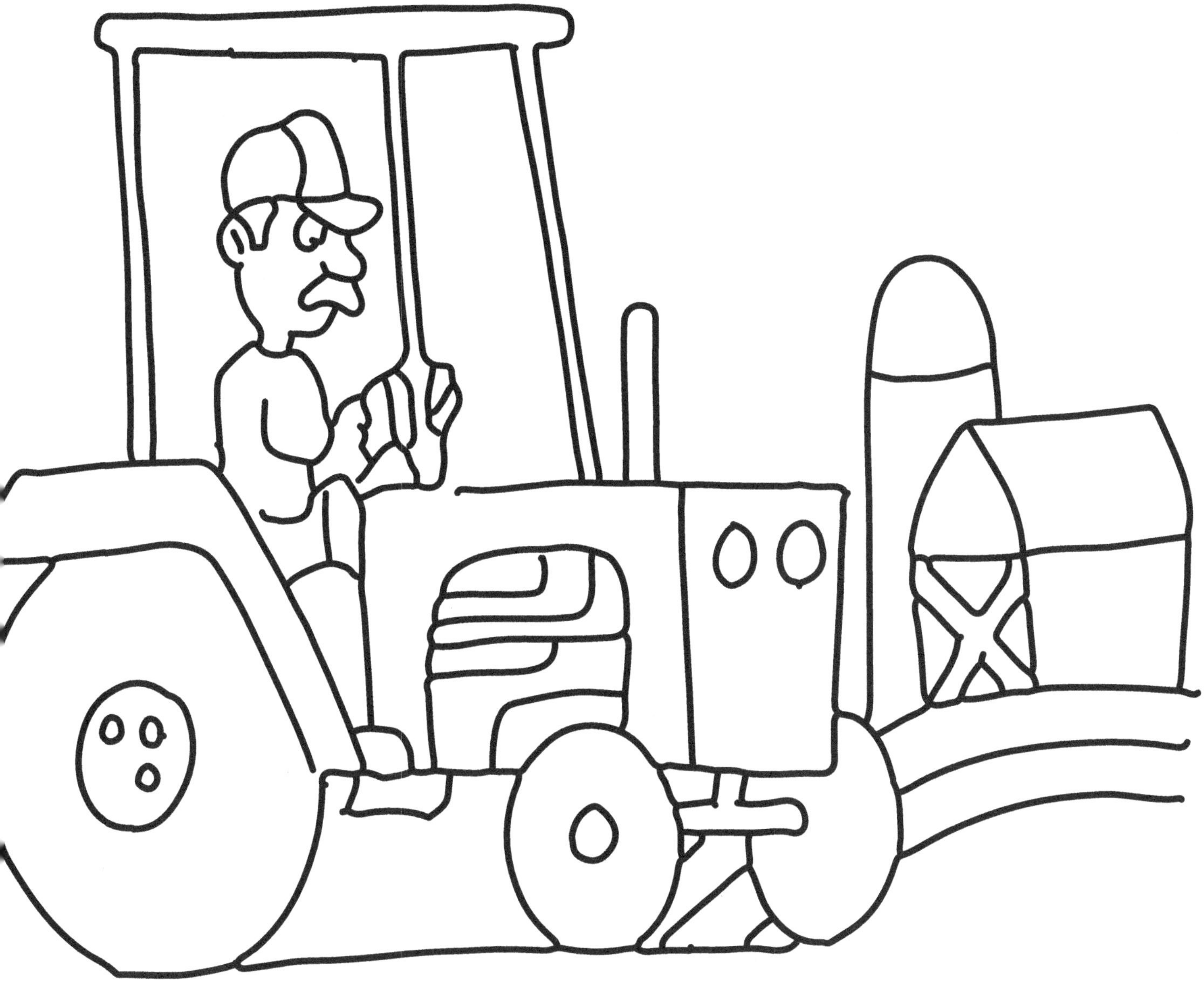

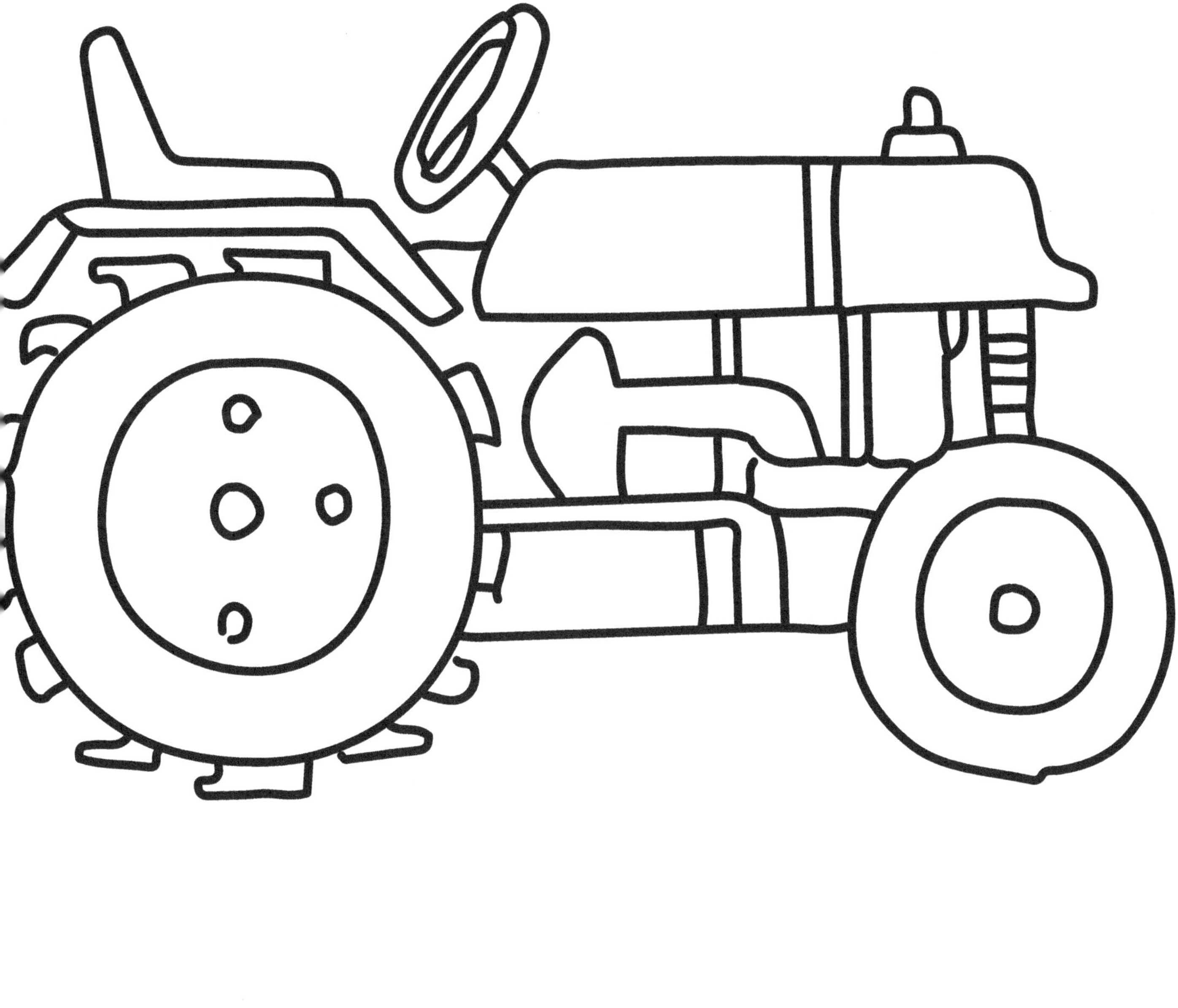

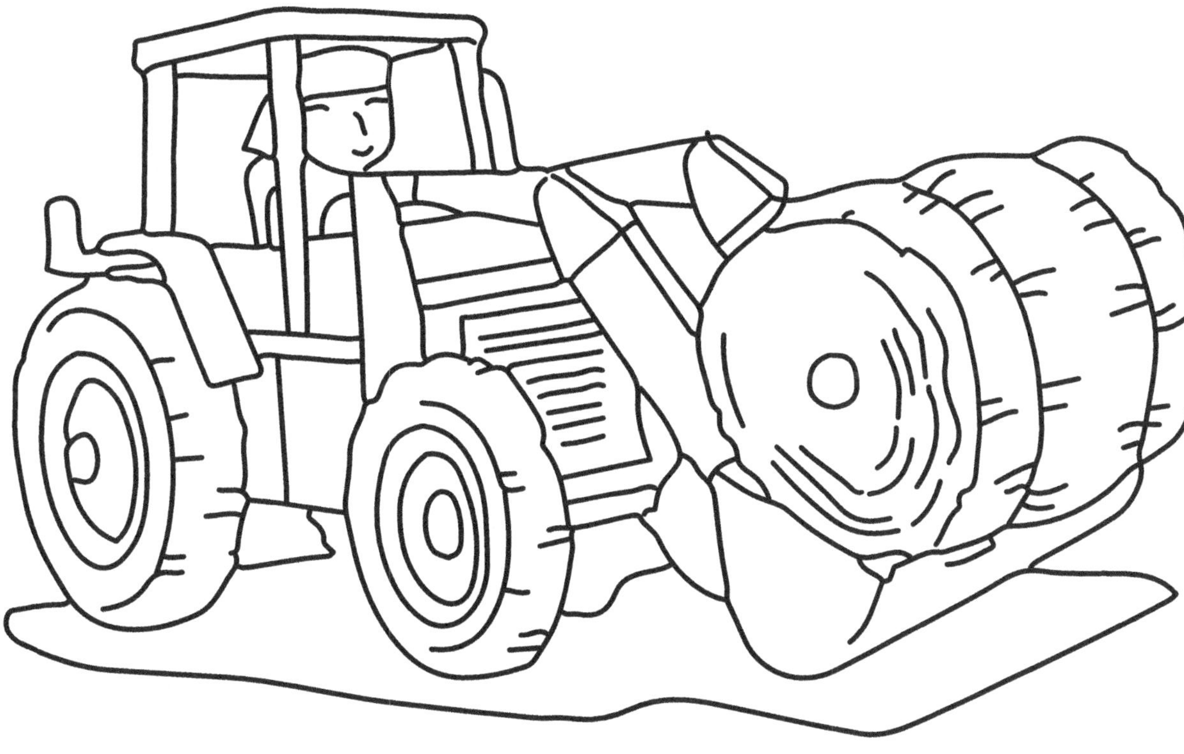

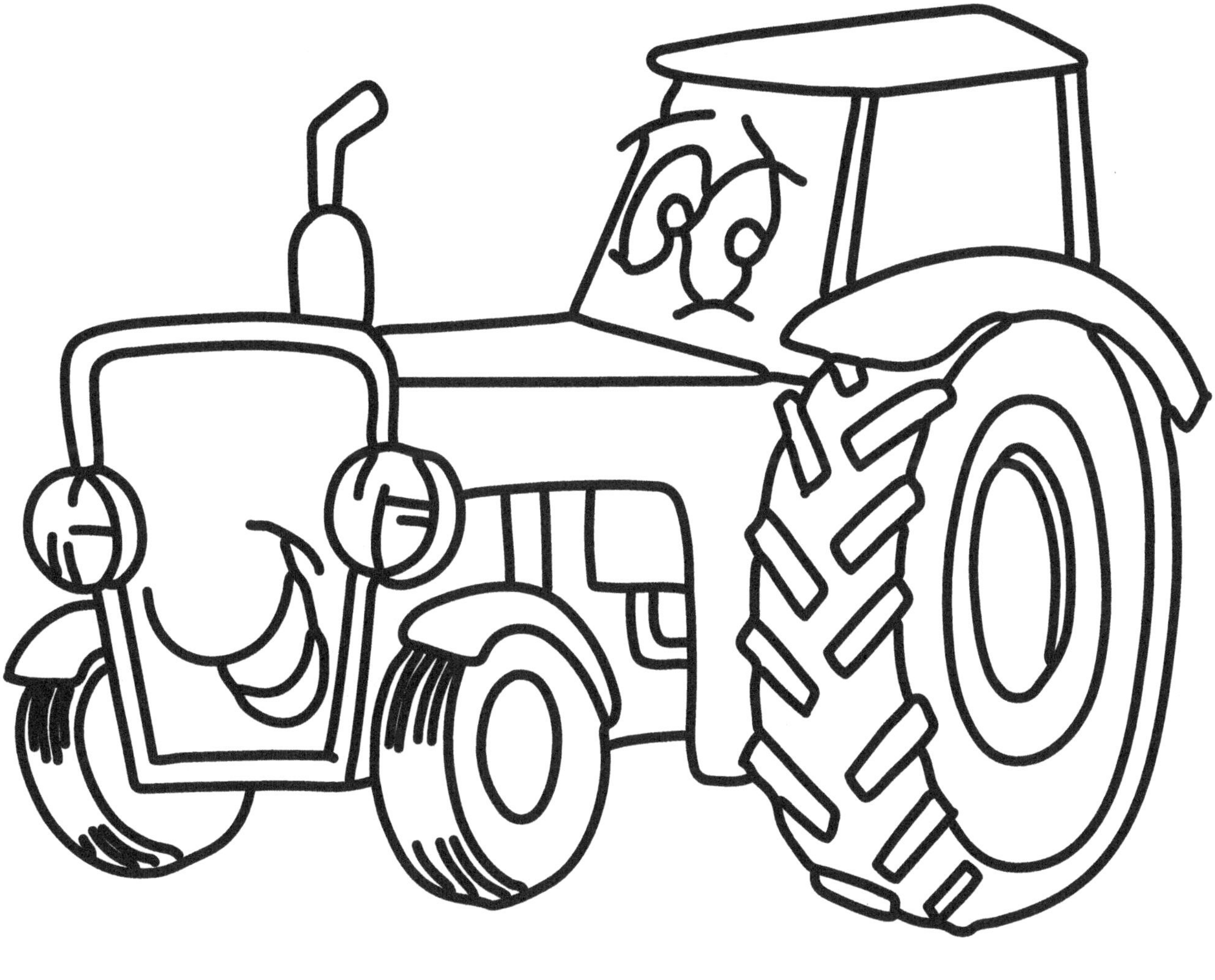

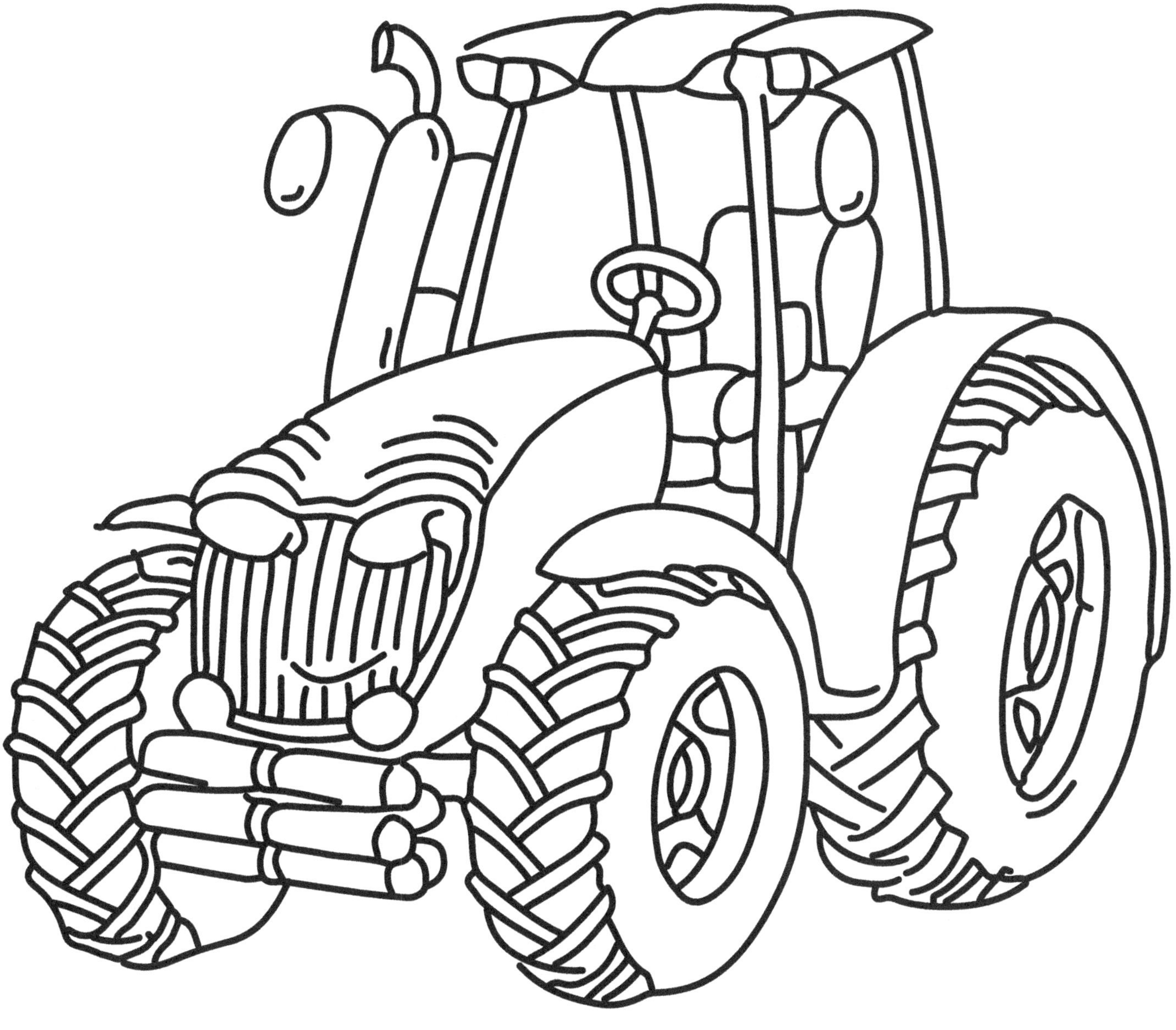

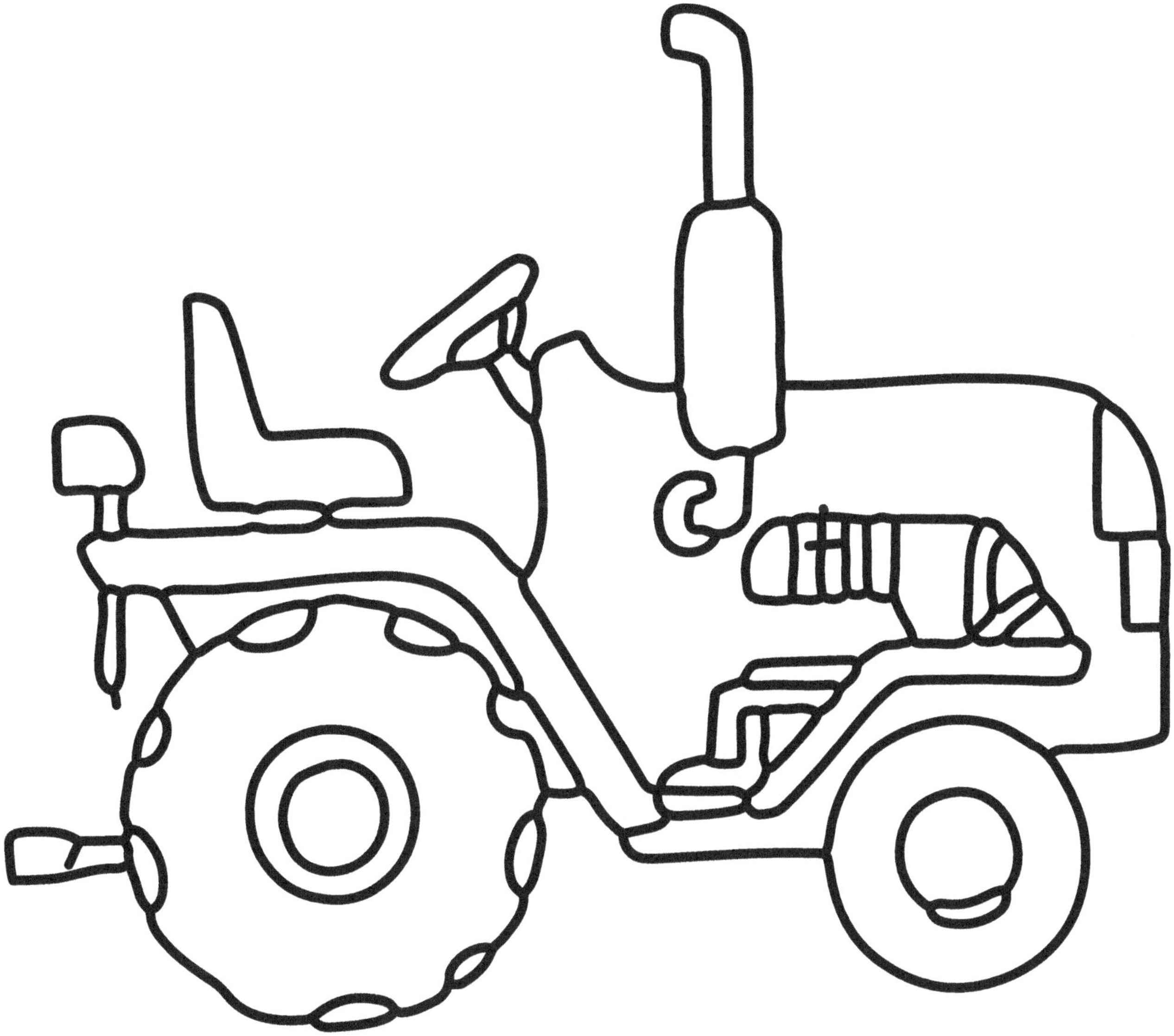

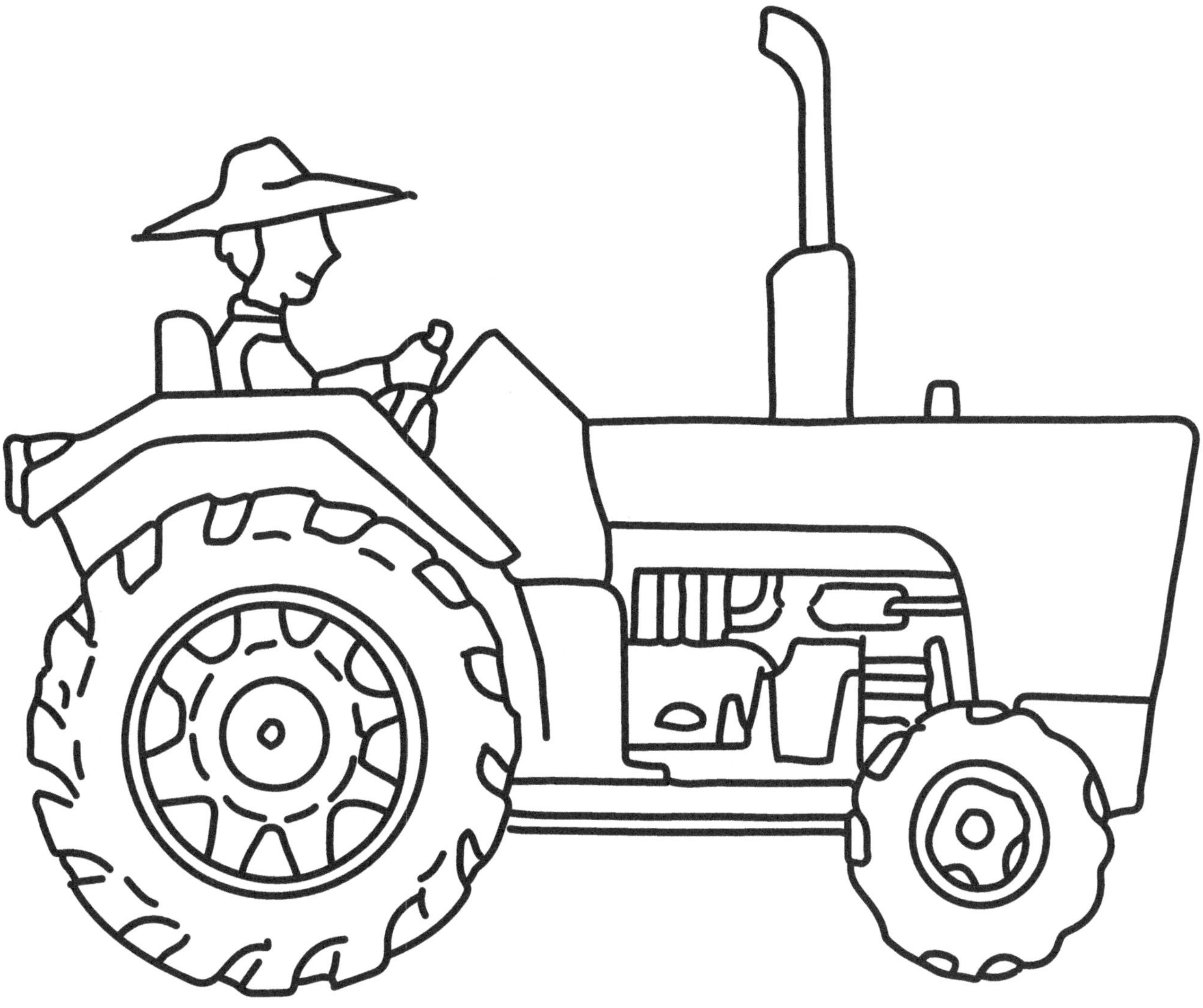

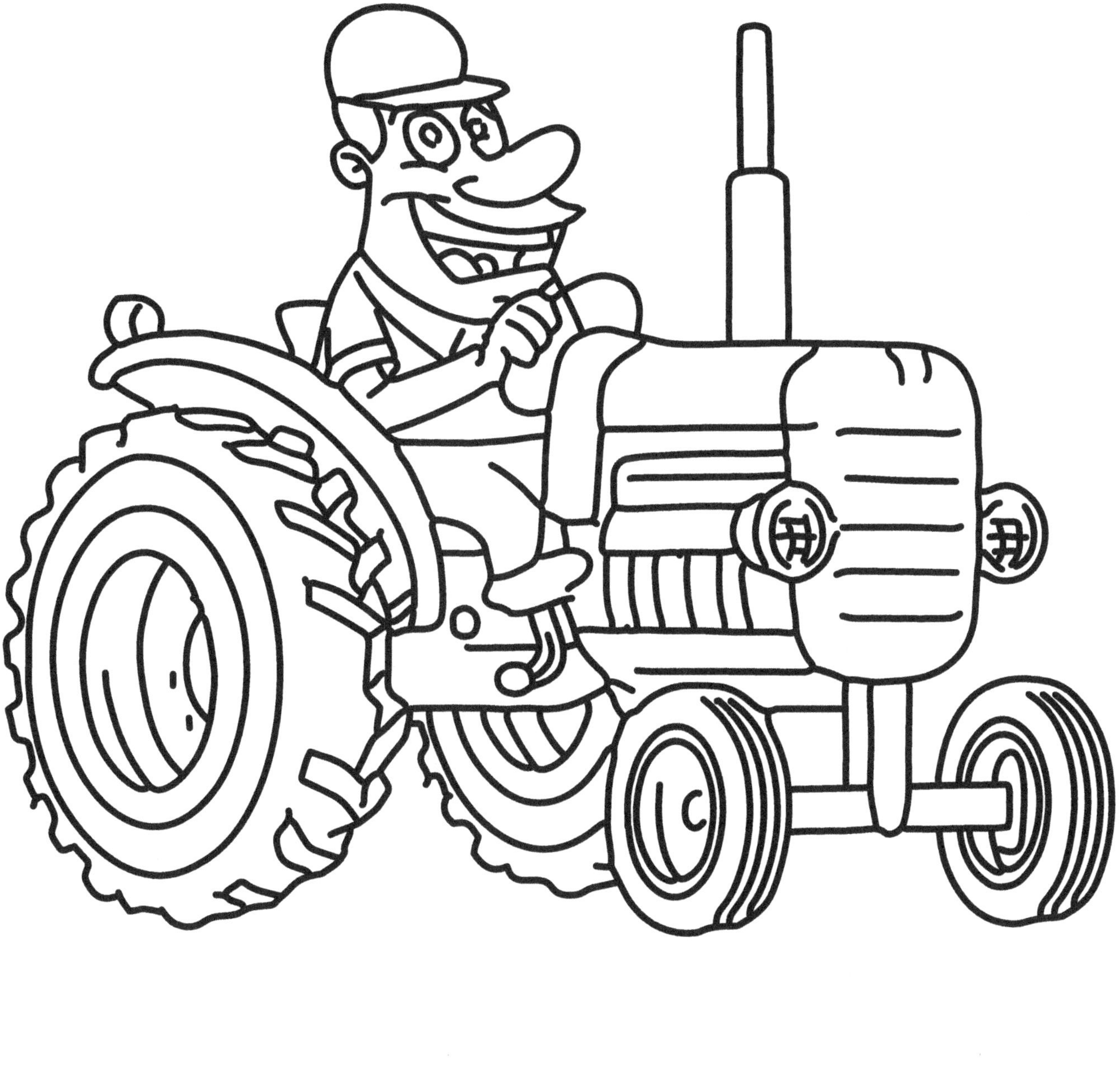

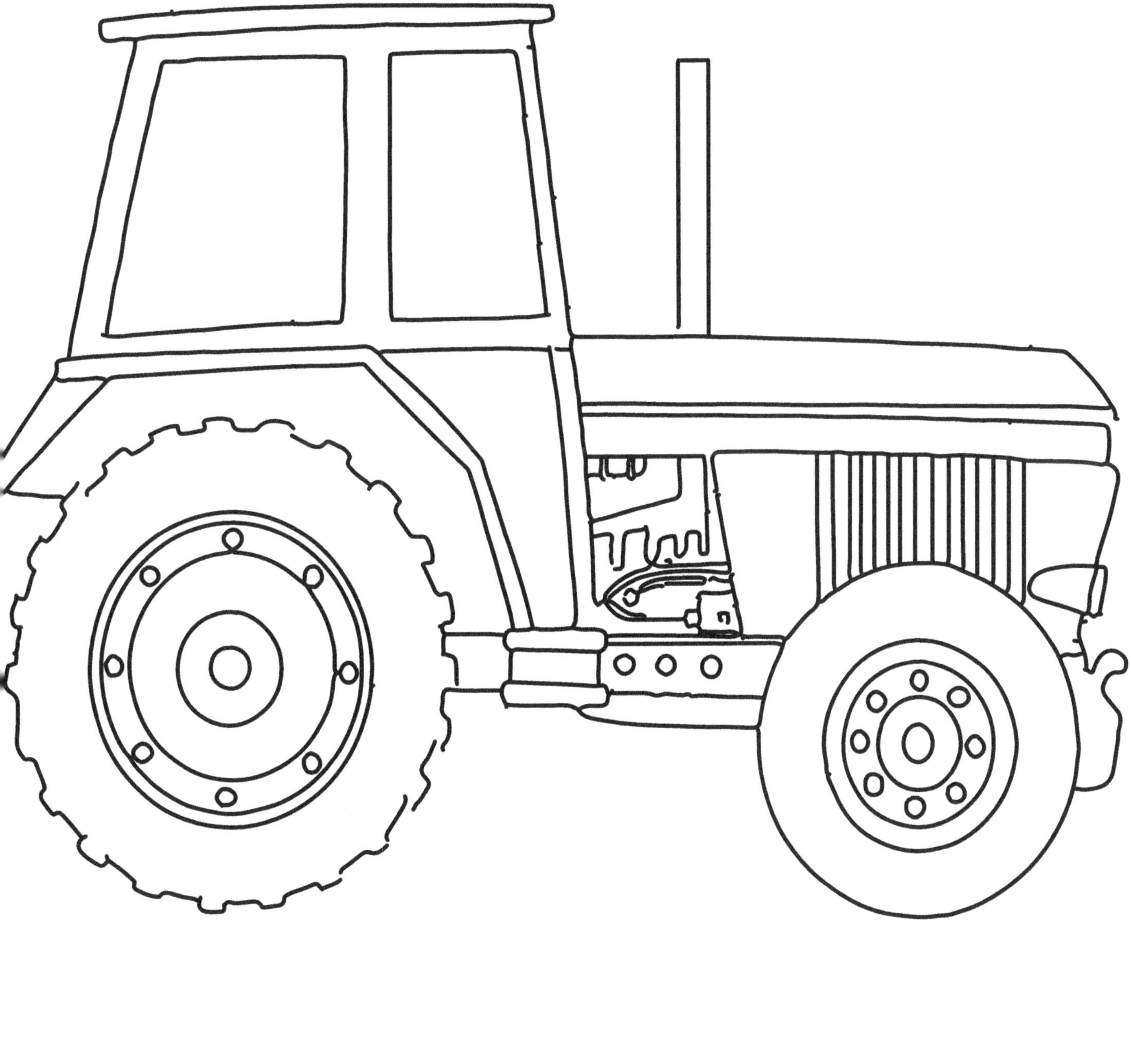

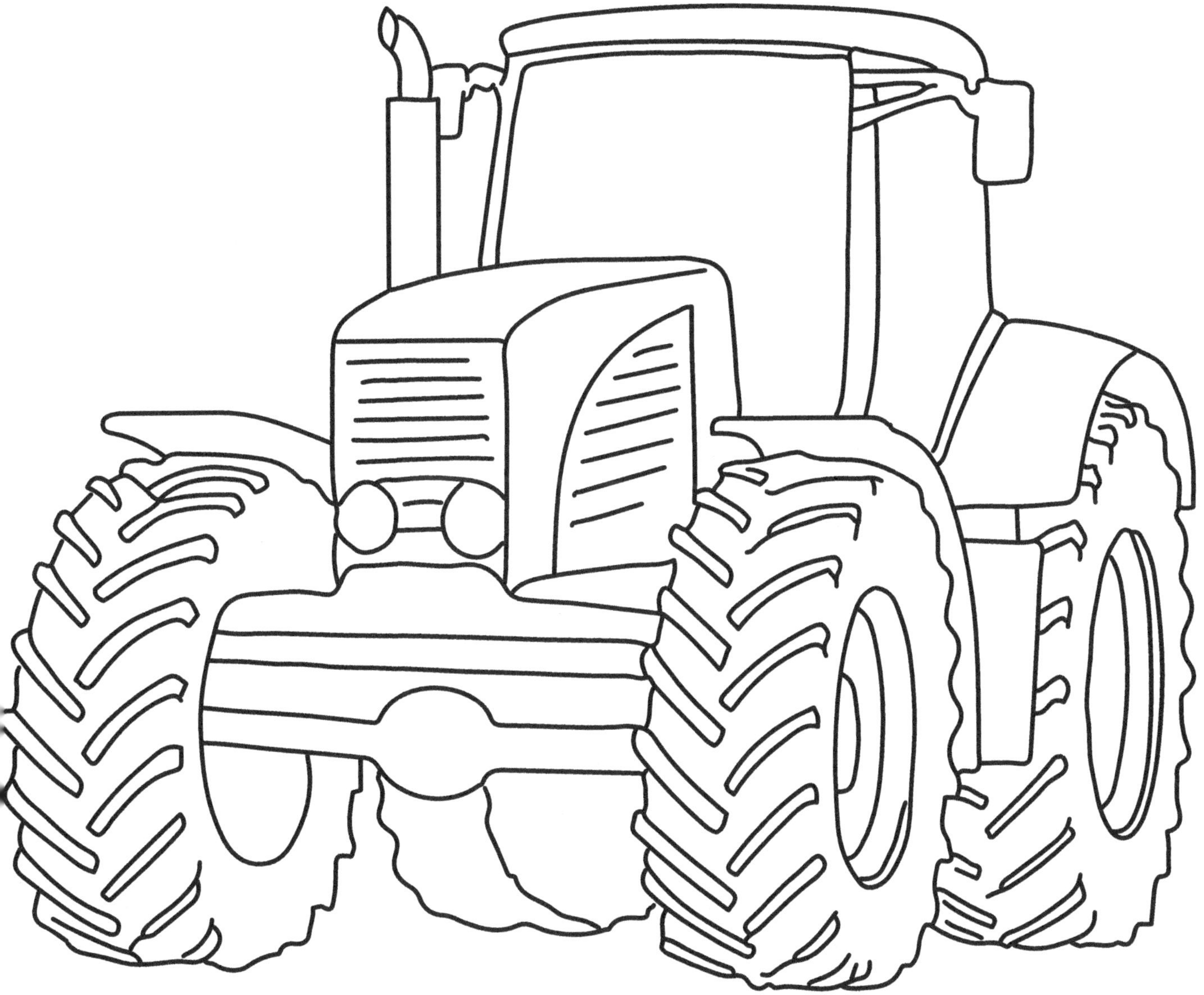

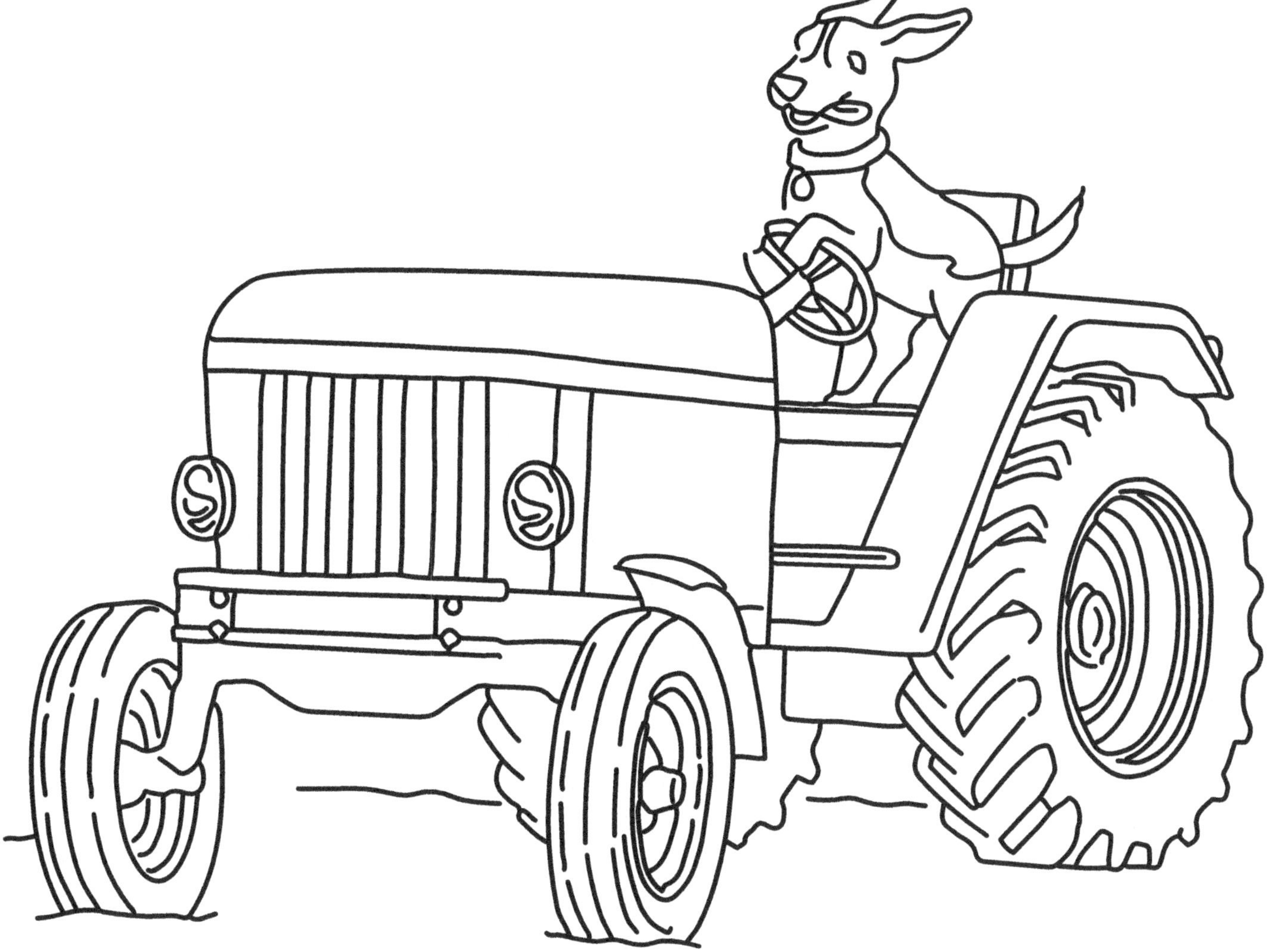

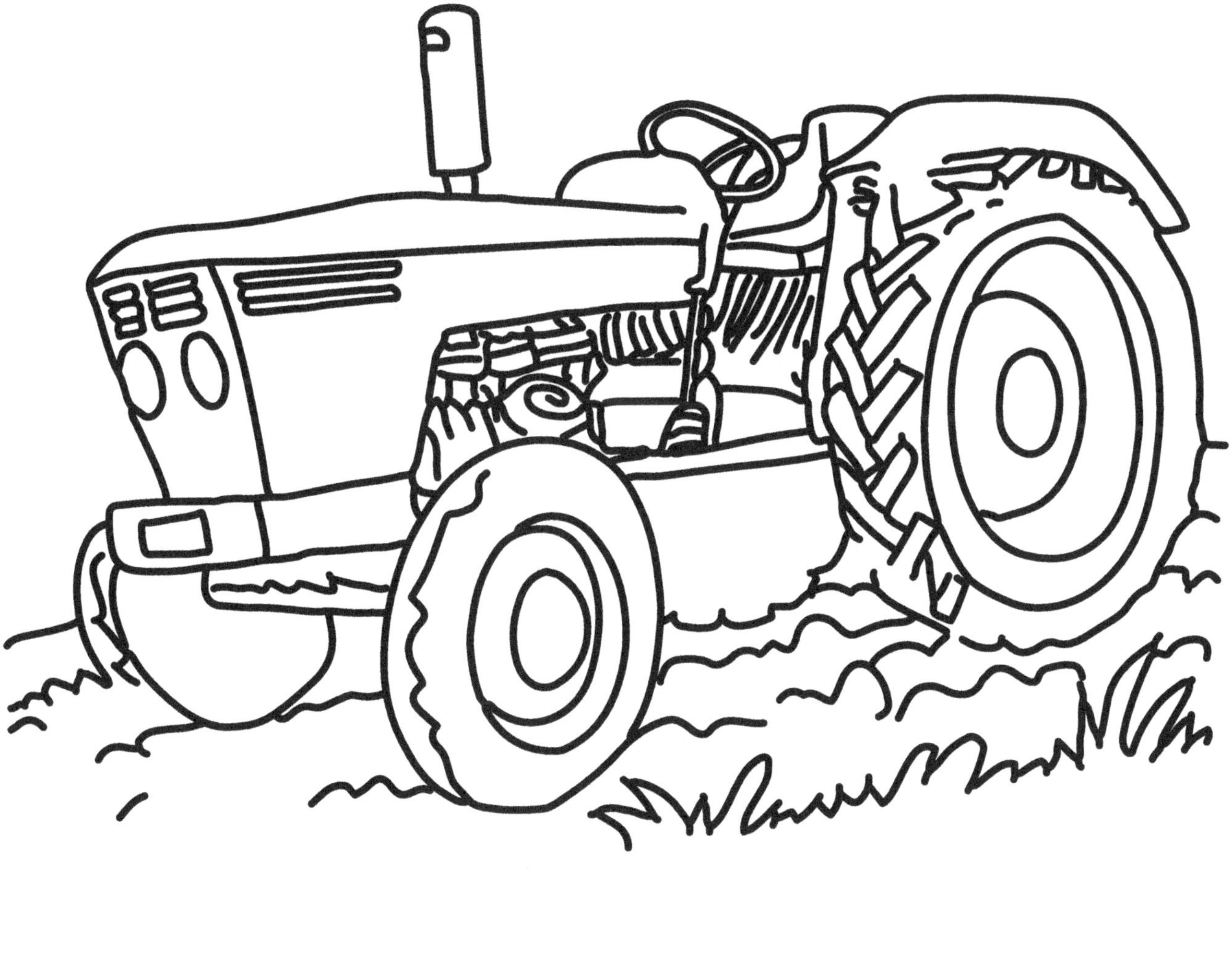

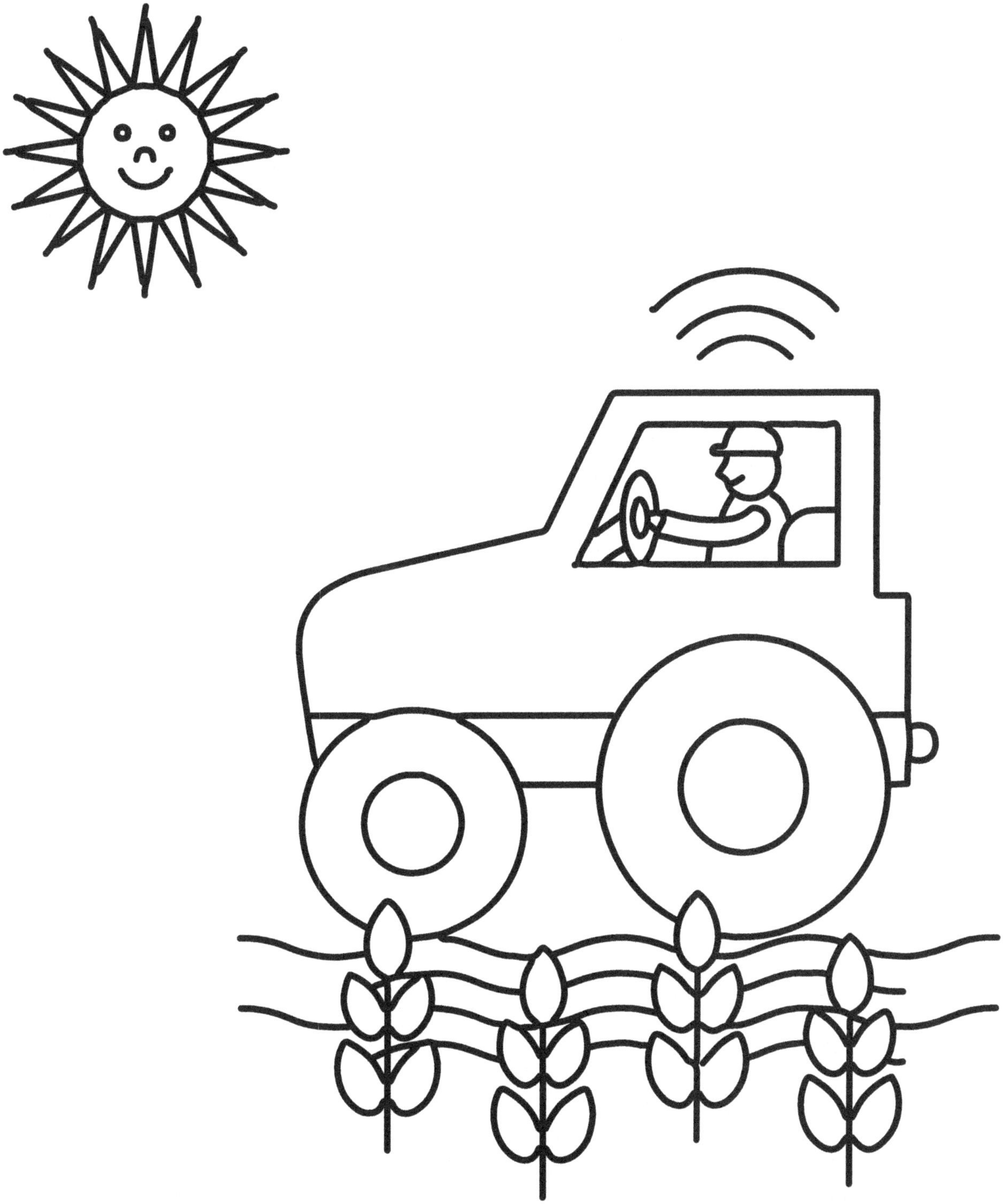

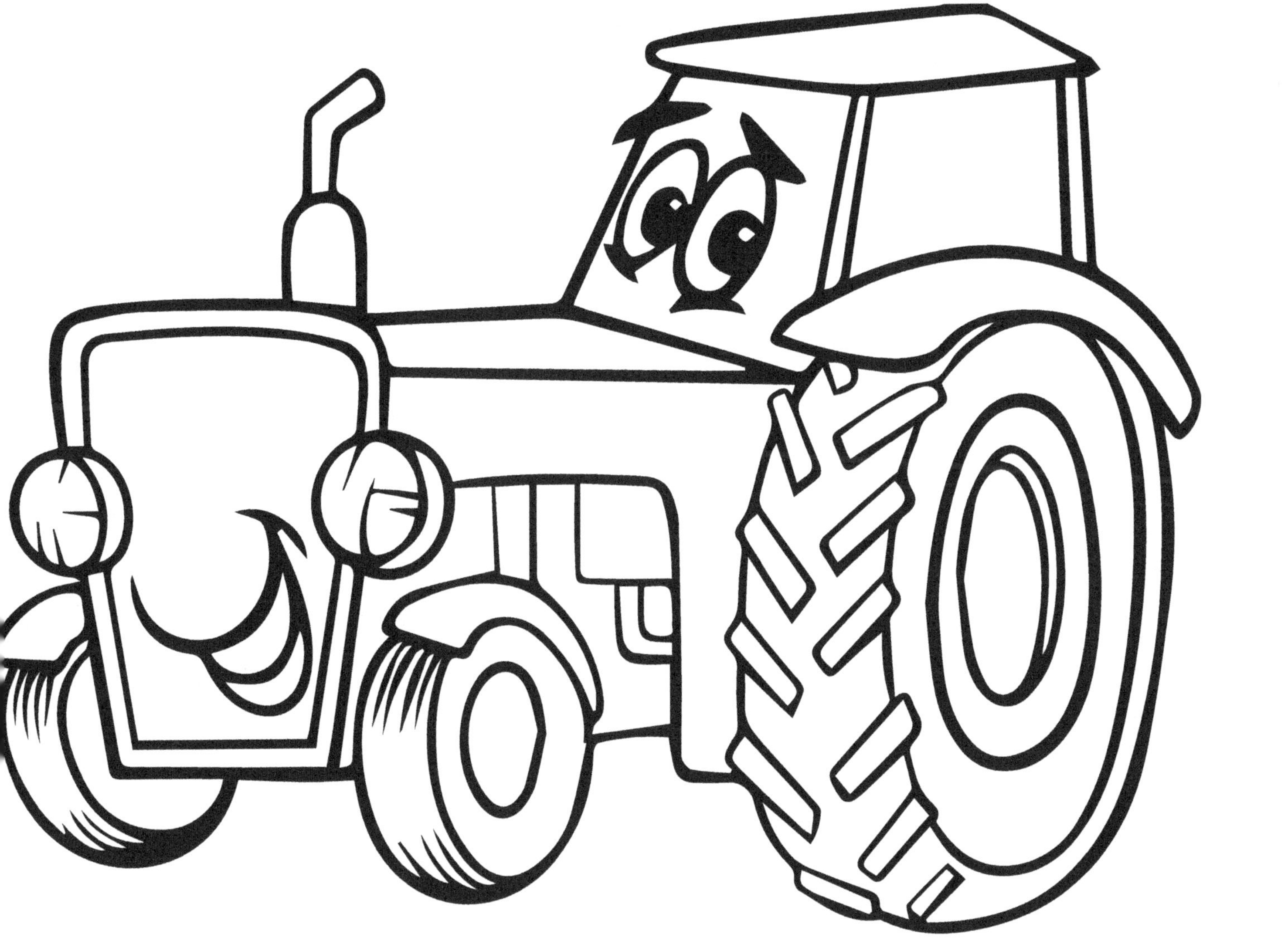

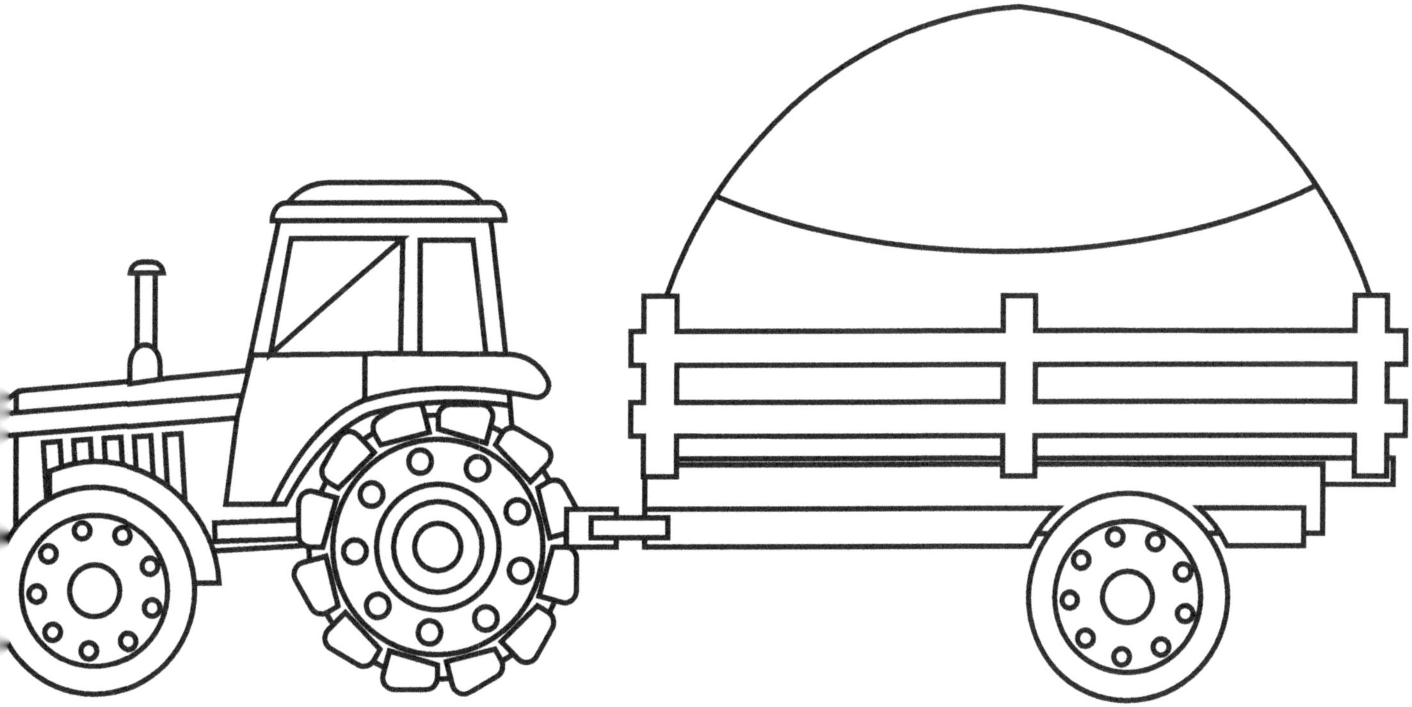

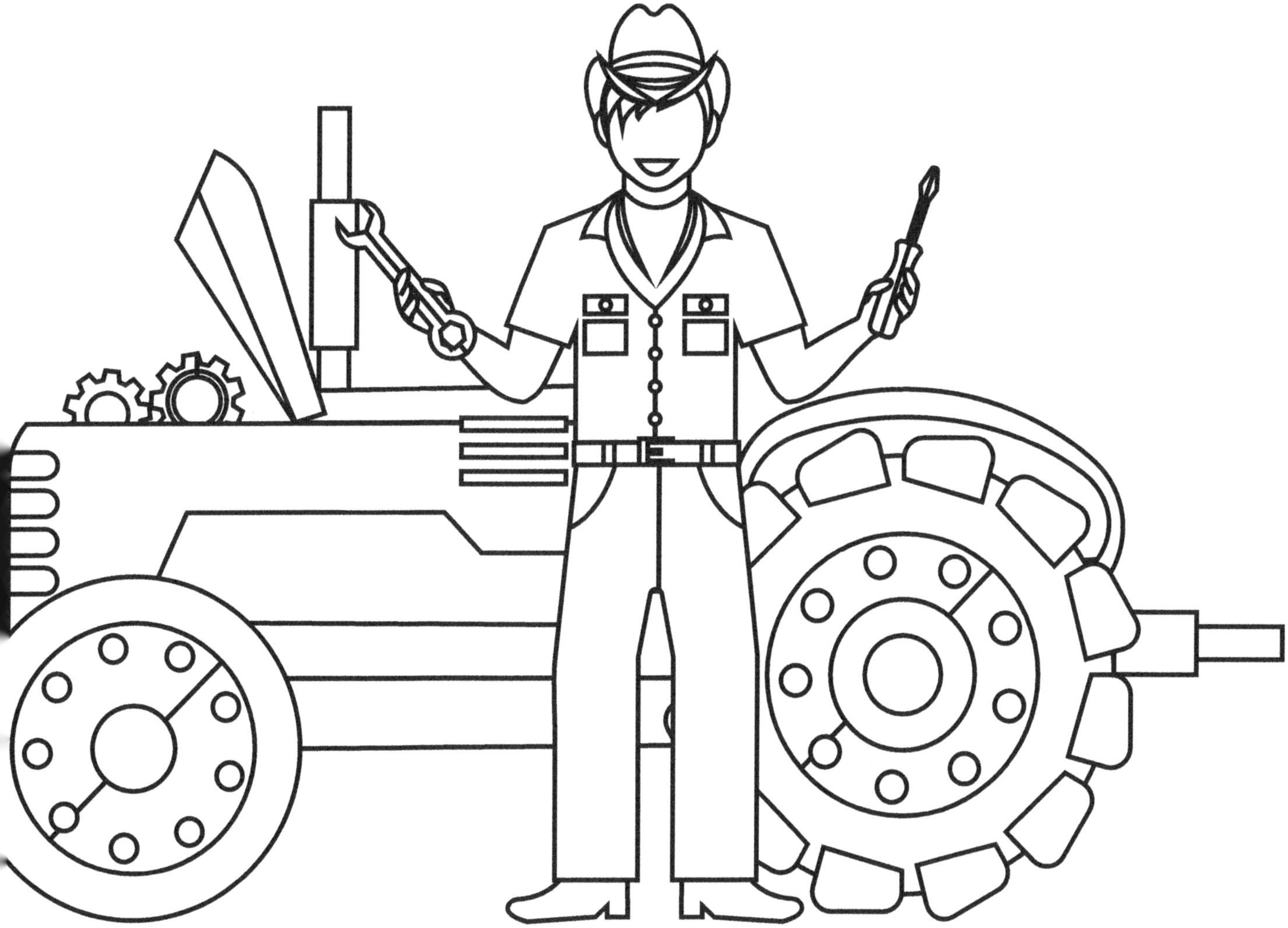

Made in the USA
Las Vegas, NV
16 February 2022

44074109R00037